GOSPEL MESSAGE AND HUMAN CULTURES

Institute for
World Concerns Series

Hervé Carrier

GOSPEL MESSAGE

AND HUMAN CULTURES

FROM LEO XIII TO JOHN PAUL II

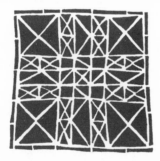

Translated by John Drury

 Duquesne University Press

Pittsburgh, Pennsylvania

Published in French under the title
Évangile et Cultures
Copyright 1987 by Libreria Editrice Vaticana

English Translation
Copyright © 1989 by Duquesne University Press

Published in the United States of America
by Duquesne University Press
600 Forbes Avenue, Pittsburgh, PA 15282

Library of Congress Cataloging-in-Publication Data

Carrier, Hervé, 1921–
    [Evangile et cultures. English]
    Gospel message and human cultures : from Leo XIII to
John Paul II
    by Hervé Carrier; translated from the French by John
Drury.
        p.   cm.
    Translation of: Evangile et cultures.
    Bibliography: p.
    Includes index.
    ISBN 0–8207–0206–4. – ISBN 0–8207–0207–2 (pbk.)
    1. Christianity and culture–History.   2. Catholic
Church–
Doctrines–History.   I. Title.
    BX1795.C85C3713   1989
    261–dc19   89–1303
                                                         CIP

Translation Note: All references and quotations,
whatever their primary source, have been
translated from the original French edition.

Contents

PART THREE
CULTURES AND THE GOSPEL MESSAGE

The Age of Human Cultures

A NEW AWARENESS OF CULTURES

In the wake of Vatican II, Christians are taking a new look at the world and its relationship to the gospel message. One of the privileged areas of their involvement is the realm of human culture, now regarded as the new locus of the Church.

This book seeks to point up the contribution, of Vatican II and the popes, from Leo XIII to John Paul II, to the growth of Christian awareness with respect to the subject. I should like to show how a "cultural conscientization," if I might call it that, was fostered among Christians between the time of Leo XIII and Vatican II. With Paul VI and the Synod of Bishops that inspired the exhortation *Evangelii Nuntiandi* (1975), the meeting of gospel message and living cultures became a priority for the Church. It is also a central concern of John Paul II. As he never tires of repeating, the Church's dialogue with present-day cultures is of crucial importance for the world's future.

We shall see how this maturation of evangelical dialogue has profited from more recent theological and sociological reflection, reflection that has put Catholics in deeper fellowship with their times and prompted them to adopt the methods of cultural analysis, thus giving better definition to their service to humankind and their evangelizing activity in the world. This new sensitivity to cultures merits our total attention.

THE RISE OF CULTURES TO PROMINENCE

One of the most astonishing developments of our age is, in fact, the rise of cultures to prominence. Never before has the reality of culture been so vigorously asserted in the lives of individuals and societies. With the decline and decay of ideologies and utopias, it is the human being itself that is now seeking its identity anew as subject and actor. This radicalism, which I have called a "cultural conscientization," holds out great promise and, at the same time, points to underlying uneasiness.

On the one hand, culture expresses a fundamental need for identity, dignity, and free participation in the benefits of civilization. Memory as well as project, culture constitutes the ideal norm—that which spurs the human being to move ahead and excel in fruitful ways. With the rise of new nations and the present media revolution, cultural progress henceforth seems to be the major aspiration of every man and every woman. And let me stress right away that this aspiration is inextricably bound up with the social, economic, and political development of peoples. The rise of cultures to prominence, then, promises a more humanized and shared future, a future more respectful of the creative values of the spirit. Promoting the culture of persons and defending the cultural identity of peoples has become the major challenge facing us and our community commitments. Here a vast field has opened up for the responsibility of persons and institutions, and of Christians especially.

On the other hand, there is another side to be considered— namely, that the cultures of our time, though bearing the loftiest of values, are often accompanied by internal contradictions that could prove fatal for the communities that incarnate them. This is a disquieting fact, as I have already noted, and it manifests itself in many ways. On one front we note the exasperation of traditional cultures that are threatened with breakup in the face of a badly assimilated modernization or a pluralism devoid of some minimal consensus; and these same tensions are also being experienced within more than one community of believers. On another front we see new nations being exhausted by their disparate battles against the cultural domination of the powerful. On still another front we see massive immigration upsetting the cultural equilibrium of host countries and creating problems of coexistence that are poorly defined and far from being solved. Our even more recent experience tells us that aggravated cultural tensions can lead to seemingly endless wars. Finally, in countries ruled by authoritarian regimes, there is a sharp clash between the officially proclaimed ideology and the living culture of their populations. This drama has been going on in several nations of Eastern Europe for at least forty years.

THE IMPORTANCE OF CULTURAL UNDERSTANDING AND DIALOGUE

In the following pages I shall try to show how the Church has placed itself at the very heart of these cultural concerns. The Church is aware of the crucial importance of cultural understanding and dialogue between cultures, for the destiny of humanity is at stake. One could rightly say that our era has become the "age of cultures." Social observation makes clear that two major concerns occupy our contemporaries.

First, they are asking themselves questions about their *cultural identity*, given that they live in a world where the landmarks of the past are being blurred by the rapid, worldwide changes sweeping our societies. How are they to remain themselves with dignity and liberty in the face of a present that is threatened and a future yet to be fashioned? All human collectivities must now redefine their essential traits in a continually changing socio-cultural context.

Secondly, this reaffirmation of their cultural identities cries out for *dialogue* between cultures because all human beings are becoming aware of their ever-increasing interdependence. No group can live isolated within itself; the price would be total exhaustion and impoverishment. The world of the future will be able to exist only in a culture of solidarity, sole pledge of justice, peace, and development for all.

Hence the Church sees culture as the privileged terrain of its activity, by bringing to culture the values of the gospel message, or simply by trying to defend the human being and its radical dignity. To our generation the Church proclaims that it is essentially through their culture that human beings can survive and progress, hence that the future of humanity depends upon culture.

In the present-day world the Church stands out as one of the rare entities capable of undertaking the defense of the human being as such in a wholly free and disinterested way. It is becoming increasingly clear that there is a connaturalness between the Church, the human being, and culture.

PRIORITY QUESTIONS

Among the countless problems arising on the horizon of cultures today I shall focus on a series of questions that seem to merit priority attention from our contemporaries, and from Christians in particular. Here are the principal questions and issues I shall be considering.

How has the concept of *culture* taken an anthropological meaning and how has it become both an instrument of *social analysis* and
a *category of action* for the development of societies?

How has the Church come to *modernize its concept of culture*? Why
has the expression "Christian civilization," used so frequently up
to 1950, gradually given way to the concept of culture?

Faced with *cultures that are threatened or shattered*, how can
Christians involve themselves in the defense of human beings and
their culture? I shall try to show that the *fight for culture* is inextricably bound up with the *fight for justice*.

I shall also consider under what ethical preconditions the development of cultures can benefit from the intervention of governments, the majority of which now pursue a *cultural policy*.

Looking more directly at the specific activity of the Church, I
shall consider the term *"evangelization of cultures,"* used more and
more frequently over the last fifteen years, and try to pinpoint its
precise meaning. I shall focus especially on the issue of *"inculturation,"* which has become more and more central in current debates
about the insertion of the gospel in the cultures of our day. To
complete this picture, I shall examine *experiences of inculturation*
actually being lived through by Christians in countries newly
evangelized or reevangelized.

Within the Church itself Christians must live with a situation of
cultural pluralism, which sometimes produces tensions, misunderstandings, and conflicts. Hence there is a need to explore the
relationship between *pluralism* and *universality* within the ecclesial
community.

Finally, I shall focus on "cultural" questions in the more traditional and classic sense of the term. I shall consider how the
Church today stands vis-à-vis the realm of *science and the arts*.
Following a connatural vocation, as it were, the Church has made
itself the ally of the sciences and arts as signs of hope for the
progress of humanity.

The panorama of questions here raised takes us back to the
manifold dimensions of culture that we shall then examine: culture
understood in the *humanist and classic sense* and culture considered
as *lifestyle* or *living anthropology*.

Confronting that vast universe, the Church sees itself as having
two missions. One mission is to *defend and promote human culture*
simply and solely because the human being, created in the image
of God, deserves to be loved for itself. The other mission, more
specifically linked to the Christian faith, has a further objective: to

freely carry *the gospel message into cultures* so that they may be able to grow to their full potential and to transcend themselves in hope. There we have the stimulating and complicated challenge facing us in the encounter between the Church and cultures.

Here I must thank Sister Maryvonne Duclaux, RSCJ, for her competent help in every phase of putting together this work. Her assistance was valuable to me both in researching documentation and in elaborating the written text.

PART ONE

CULTURE AS THE NEW LOCUS FOR CHURCH ACTION

Our age is characterized by a new *perception* of *culture,* and modern thought uses the method of *cultural analysis* to gain a better understanding of the concrete situation of the men and women of our time.

In the following two chapters we shall see how the Church has adopted this *cultural approach* in its examination of the contemporary world (chap. 1). And I shall try to pinpoint the *main stages* in the Church's growing understanding of culture and cultures (chap. 2).

1/The Church's Encounter with Modern Culture

Following the course by which the Church has come to modernize its perception of culture will be very enlightening for our inquiry in this volume. It is a development of considerable importance for the Church and its action on societies. We will see how a "cultural conscientization" has developed among Christians. Vatican II marks a turning point, to be sure: it was the first ecumenical council to deal explicitly with human culture and with the cultures of our day. But Christians had already familiarized themselves with cultural analysis, thanks to the methods of Catholic Action and religious sociology as well as with the practice of the human sciences. They had enlarged their classic conception of culture and turned their attention to the living cultures that were calling out to the Church.

To appreciate this progress in the understanding of societies, I shall first consider how the sociology of culture took shape and how its socio-historical approach has left its mark on the collective psychology of us all, and there can be no doubt that this has enriched the Church's perception of itself and the world.

CULTURE: A NEW PERCEPTION OF THE HUMAN BEING

Let me begin with a telling observation: culture occupies an increasingly important place in social discourse. The cultural factor imposes itself upon us as the first and primary datum of our whole collective life. Culture is now perceived as the fundamental dynamism conditioning every form of social, economic, political, and international life.

At the level of social representation culture has become an indispensable concept for better understanding collective phe-

3

nomena and giving clearer definition to social intervention; it cannot be overlooked by either sociologists or those who hold responsible positions in society. The modern notion of culture is the new paradigm, the conceptual tool, that guides our analysis of the social arena and our understanding of its vital dynamisms.

As I shall show in this book, the Church itself now uses the language of cultural analysis to diagnose social realities and to translate the gospel message of fellowship, charity, and justice into the language of present-day cultures.

The interest of our contemporaries for questions of culture is a relatively recent attitude in human history, but the reality of culture itself is obviously not new. Culture has existed since the beginnings of Homo sapiens. It is culture that has made us human beings in the proper sense. What is new is the *perception* of culture as an anthropological reality. Culture reveals to us the characteristic traits of a human collectivity: its mentality, its lifestyle, its own peculiar way of humanizing its milieu. For us, culture is the distinctive mark of a society, a social category, or a human community; and so we talk about the culture of the working class, of rural areas, of the young, of migrants, of ethnic groups, and so forth.

Before the beginning of this century the word "culture" was hardly used in this socio-historical sense. Its connotations were then *intellectual* and *esthetic*, referring to erudition, refinement of spirit, artistic and literary improvement. The concept applied to so-called cultured individuals or societal groups. This classic or humanist meaning of the term "culture" is still around today, but now the term has a *sociological* and *historical* meaning. Our present-day language bears witness to this development in such expressions as "cultural identity," "dialogue between cultures," "cultural domination," and "cultural liberation." And the Church talks about the "evangelization of cultures" and "inculturation."

I shall now spell out the anthropological meaning given to the term "culture" by modern thought and try to see what influences underlay this new development.

A DESCRIPTIVE DEFINITION OF CULTURE

Culture is the humanized universe created wittingly or unwittingly by a human collectivity. It is the group's own representation of the past and its plan for the future, its typical institutions and creations, its habits and beliefs, its characteristic attitudes and behavior patterns, its original mode of communicating, working, celebrating, and creating the techniques and works that reveal its soul and its ultimate values. Culture is the typical mentality adopted by every individual who identifies with a collectivity; it is the human heritage transmitted from generation to generation. Every community enjoying a certain permanence possesses a culture of its own: a nation, a region, a tribe, or a specific social category (such as youth or the working class). Culture designates their characteristic way of behaving, thinking, judging, perceiving themselves and being perceived by others. Each groups has its own attitudes and scales of values.

We should realize that culture, being a phenomenon of collective psychology, contains a large dose of the unconscious and the unspoken: aspects that outside observers can often perceive more keenly than can the group under observation. One is reminded of Montesquieu's astonished reaction and question: "So-and-so is a Persian. How extraordinary! How can a person be a Persian?" Increased travel abroad and the worldwide media of electronic communication have made us profoundly sensitive to the diversity of human mentalities, customs, and lifestyles, revealing to us the human richness subsumed under the expression "cultural diversity."

Let us then recall that the word "culture" has two meanings. One is the older classic or humanist meaning that we apply to "cultured persons"; the other is the more modern, anthropological meaning we use to designate the collective psychology and typical lifestyles of a human group. Let us also note that culture, understood in the older, classic sense, generally has a normative connotation: culture alludes to an ideal that is to be attained. Culture understood in the more modern anthropological sense, on the other hand, is primarily a descriptive notion: culture describes a socio-historical or socio-cultural situation which, like every human reality, embodies both positive and negative elements vis-à-vis the ideal norm or the loftiest culture of humanity.

In an earlier day, authors tended to set these two meanings of the word "culture" in opposition to each other; today we more clearly appreciate the perduring interrelationships operative between the culture of the individual and the culture of the collectivity, between the culture of the learned and the living culture of ordinary persons. I shall return to this issue, but right now I shall consider the gradual growth of the modern concept of culture and the use of a cultural approach in the study of social phenomena.

EMERGENCE OF THE CONCEPT OF CULTURE

It was in and through the slow maturation of the socio-historical sciences that there developed the method of cultural analysis, a method now used by modern sociologists and the Church in trying to perceive social realities and act within cultures. Let me briefly note the main stages in the emergence of the modern concept of culture.

In the nineteenth century, observers of so-called primitive societies had introduced the term "culture" to analyze the ways, customs, and social habits of ethnic groups. According to this outlook, the culture of primitive societies was somehow the counterpart of the civilization of more advanced peoples. In 1871 anthropologist Edward Tylor published his work entitled *Primitive Culture*. In it we find one of the first definitions of culture in the anthropological sense. "Culture or civilization is that complex whole which includes knowledge, belief, art, morals, law, custom, and any other capabilities and habits acquired by man as a member of society."[1]

A less well-known and perhaps less striking source, yet a hardly negligible one, comes out of the German tradition. Let me mention specifically Samuel Pufendorf (1632–94), lawyer and son of a minister, who was one of the pioneers of the idea of culture in Germany. He set forth an anthropology that differentiated biological entities (*entia physica*) and moral entities (*entia moralia*) in society. Human society, he wrote was basically explained by moral entities, which were grounded on the dignity and freedom of the human being, and carried the human being into all the forms of sociality. Institutions are endowed with an objective life, but they all are based on acts of moral will by individuals. Pufendorf affirmed the central role of culture in society, for individuals had an obligation to cultivate their being. "Culture is necessary for the human being": *homini cultura sui est necessaria.*[2] Pufendorf published several works. We may note in particular here his work entitled *Officio Hominis et Civis* (the duties of the human being and the citizen), which was very influential in Europe and inspired the *Declaration of the Rights of the Human Being and the Citizen* issuing from the French Revolution of 1789.[3]

In England the idea of culture surfaced in social discourse around the beginning of the nineteenth century. As Raymond Williams notes, five basic terms came into currency in English at that time: industry, democracy, class, art, and culture. The most striking of those five terms is "culture," in his opinion, because it gives notice of changes that characterize the new age.[4]

We should also note the influence of Karl Marx on the notion of culture, particularly on the notion of "proletarian culture" that was picked up later by Lenin. In his interpretation of social reality Marx stressed the phenomenon of cultural domination, showing how subordinate classes are dominated by the culture of those classes controlling the means of production.[5]

All these currents of thought from different sources helped to shape the modern concept of culture. At first the term was used only by specialists, writers, and anthropologists, mainly those in England, Germany, France, and the United States. After World War I the word gradually seeped into common parlance as a thought-category for analyzing modern societies. Social upheavals and new mind-sets after the war provided ample material for observation; and public opinion was vividly sensitized to the changes sweeping over institutions, values, and the lifestyles of societies increasingly marked by pluralism. Thus, industrial societies became, in turn, objects of cultural analysis.

In our own day the clash of cultures takes place before our very eyes. We are witnessing dramatic confrontations between nationalisms often raised to the pitch of fanaticism, various religious fundamentalisms, and lifestyles that often set us in radical opposition to each other. It is now clear that the crucial issue has to do with culture and we are being invited, almost against our wishes, to undertake *cultural analysis*. We all must shoulder the inescapable necessity of intercultural dialogue, if for no other reason than to ensure the survival of human beings and societies.

This development merits two remarks. First, we can say that culture is now an operational term for analyzing social reality and acting on it. Culture has become a dynamic category, as various expressions suggest: cultural policy, cultural action, cultural revolution, cultural liberation. As I noted above, the Church itself gives a dynamic connotation to the word "culture" when it speaks of the evangelization of cultures, encounter between cultures, and inculturation.

Secondly, we now have a better appreciation of the dialectical relationship between the culture of the individual and that of the community to which he or she belongs. In an age when schooling is tending to become universal, it is more difficult than ever before to oppose "elite culture" to the culture lived by the people. The modern media have contributed greatly both to the personalization and the socialization of culture. The intensification of communications between all sectors of society and all parts of the world has spurred everyone to take cognizance of the diversity evident in human ways of living; and it is prompting each and every human group to ask questions about its own identity. This explains why our contemporaries are turning their attention to the reality of culture, the diversity of cultures, dialogue between cultures, and the defense of cultural particularities. The modern human spirit is trying to better understand what culture is and what sort of dynamic role it plays in the life of individuals and societies.

For its part, the Church has clearly made this modern conception of culture its own, as is particularly evident from Vatican II on. The conciliar document *Gaudium et Spes* offers a definition of culture that perfectly harmonizes the two dimensions, classic and anthropological, I stressed above:

> In the broad sense the word "culture" designates all those things whereby the human being refines and develops the manifold capabilities of its spirit and its body; whereby it tries to bring the universe under control through knowledge and work; whereby it humanizes social life, both family life and civic life as a whole, thanks to the progress of customs and institutions; whereby, finally, over the course of time it expresses, communicates, and preserves in its works the great spiritual experiences and major aspirations of humanity, so that they may promote the progress of many, of the whole human race even.
>
> It follows, then, that human culture necessarily entails a historical and social aspect, and that the word "culture" often takes on a sociological and even ethnological sense.[6]

MODERNIZATION OF THE CHURCH'S VIEW OF CULTURE

The concillar document *Gaudium et Spes* marks a new stage in the social teaching of the Church. For the first time a Church council attempted to deal systematically with the historical situation of the world and the condition of contemporary human beings. Some who witnessed Vatican II do not hesitate to say that it was concerned essentially with two topics, the Church and today's human being, and each topic was the subject of a major constitution: *Lumen Gentium* and *Gaudium et Spes*, respectively. First, it dealt with the major theme of *the Church*: the Church's nature, the liturgy, revelation, bishops, priests, religious, laity, the Church and education, missions, the media, relationships with other Christians and with other religions. Secondly, Vatican II focused on *the world today*. The resultant document, *Gaudium et Spes*, was formulated jointly by pastors, theologians, and sociologists whose method was interdisciplinary and whose approach was clearly anthropological in trying to understand the world of our day. It has been noticed, for example, that the word "history" crops up 63 times, and the word "culture" 91 times, in the documents of Vatican II. Paul VI noted this novel aspect of the council in his closing address of December 7, 1965: "The council took a lively insterest in studying the modern world. Perhaps never before has the Church felt such a need to know, approach, understand, penetrate, serve, and evangelize the society around it; and to pursue it, so to speak, in its rapid, ongoing transformations."[7]

Perfecting methods of analysis used in its earlier social documents, the Church, especially since *Gaudium et Spes*, perceives and tries to understand social reality in terms of the typical cultures of our day. Cultural factors pervade every sphere of reality: societal life, the family, ethics, politics, economics, and international affairs. This accounts for the new, contemporary tone of Church documents that attempt to describe the social conditions of our day. A new cultural insight is leading the Church to discover that human society seems to be entering "a new order of things," as John XXIII put it at the opening of Vatican II.[8]

During Vatican II itself, Paul VI issued a pressing invitation to understand the modern world. He made himself the advocate of dialogue with every person of good will: "The Church must enter into dialogue with the world in which it lives. The Church turns itself into word . . . message . . . conversation. . . . Before converting the world, indeed in order to convert the world, the Church must approach the world and speak to it."[9] The Church, noted Paul VI, must reunite with the human as such through a kind of cultural communion. We all share this "first universality".

The Church fully shoulders the cause of humanity: "Wherever human beings are trying to understand themselves and the world, to defend justice and culture, Christians are honored to take part in that effort."[10]

It was this fruitful intuition that guided the authors of *Gaudium et Spes* in their look at today's world, and they managed to offer an overview of contemporary culture that is notable for its keenness and penetration. But Vatican II as a whole must be examined again if we are to grasp its contribution to a cultural understanding of our time, so I shall briefly consider its most important highlights in this area.

VATICAN II AS A CULTURAL HAPPENING

One of the characteristic features of Vatican II was precisely its new look at the cultures within which the Church must now operate. In its formulations about culture we find, as it were, a synthesis of the Church's earlier experiences and teachings. I shall return to that matter further on. Given the standpoint of the present chapter, I shall here try to trace the main ideas of Vatican II dealing specifically with the relationship between Christianity and culture. In particular, I shall focus on the Church's growing attention to cultural realities. *Gaudium et Spes* remains the major document on the question; but here is not the place to analyze its principal propositions, which will be considered in the course of the following chapters. Instead I shall offer a general overview of the conciliar documents as a whole.

Vatican II brought out clearly how the Church has contributed to the progress of cultures in and through its own experience. Throughout its history the Church has taken great pains to integrate itself into the most diverse cultures and to express itself through them,[11] The Church is also fully aware of its universality. It has been sent out "to all peoples of every time and place", and hence it does not identify itself with any specific culture. It remains ready and open to enter into communion with every civilization. The Church is not bound "in an exclusivist, indissoluble way to any race or nation, any particular way of life, or any customary way of life, be it ancient or modern." The Church's posture of *universality* and *communion* is doubly fruitful, enriching both the Church itself and different cultures.[12]

The Church's peculiar way of acting upon cultures is to renew human beings from within, to protect them and save them from evil. The Church "never ceases to purify and elevate the morality of peoples." Acting as a leaven, the Church makes fruitful, from within as it were, the spiritual qualities and specific gifts of every people and every age. That is the Church's way of civilizing human beings: "Thus the Church, in the very fulfillment of its own mission, already contributes thereby to the task of civilization."[13]

But Vatican II sensed the dramatic nature of the changes sweeping over societies today and understood the stakes involved in the emergent cultures. Humanity is coming to realize that it is entering a new age in history. The Church of our day must strive to understand the present-day world—its hopes, expectations, and dramas.

Profound transformations are leaving their mark on the entire globe. They were elicited by human creativity, but they also bring about changes in the human being and its ways of thinking and acting. All societies have been affected: living environments, mentalities, traditions, institutions, and customary values. As a result there are profound psychological and moral changes, and there could be serious repercussions for religion as well. Some think that the progress of learning and a critical spirit has helped to purify a magical conception of the world, but others think that the development of science might lead to a rejection of God and religion. Vatican II evaluation of scientific and technical progress was both positive and critical-minded.

True cultural progress for human beings is, in and of itself, open to the transcendent. That is why the gospel message can be productive of culture. By virtue of its mission the Church can thus contribute to the task of civilizing humanity. Culture, then, is the very dignity of human beings and their most radical need.

We can glimpse the problems that such an ideal of culture may raise. *Gaudium et Spes* enumerates some of them, which I would sum up in the following questions:

1. How is the intensification of cultural exchanges to mesh with the safeguarding of each people's patrimony and identity?

2. In particular, how are we to harmonize the culture issuing from the modern sciences with the traditional culture that is the product of the wisdom of nations and classical traditions?

3. How are we to elaborate a synthesis of increasingly specialized disciplines while taking account of the capacity for contemplation that leads to wisdom?

4. How are we to help the multitudes to share in the benefits of culture while the culture of elites continually grows and becomes more specialized?

5. How are we to recognize the autonomy of secular cultures without falling into a humanism that rejects religion?

It is in the very midst of this cultural reality that the Church now defines its evangelizing activity. It seeks to better understand the ties being woven between the faith and cultures, showing how the gospel message can be the leaven of culture. All this presupposes that Christians will display *a new perception of cultural reality* and will be spurred to act upon living cultures, seeking their inspiration in the principles of theology, and help and enlightenment from the human sciences. The Church is attentive to every trace of good it finds in the human heart or in cultures. It acts in such a way that these good things are not lost but rather "purified, elevated, and perfected for the glory of God."[14]

Lay Christians have their own proper responsibility in the task of evangelizing cultures, because their activity takes place in the very midst of civil society and living cultures. They are urged to regard the elements of the temporal order (e.g., the good things of life, the prosperity of the family, socio-economic activities, and politics) as realities with an intrinsic value of their own, not just as means or aids for the attainment of humanity's ultimate goal.[15]

It is clear, then, that the Church has the greatest respect for cultures in all their diversity and richness, but that it insists on remaining completely free to criticize them and to urge them to surpass themselves.

In its decree on mission work, *Ad Gentes*, Vatican II invites Christians to involve themselves in the cultural and social life of their country and to familiarize themselves with its national and religious traditions, "gladly and respectfully laying bare the seeds of the Word that lie hidden in them."[16] Above all, they must pay heed to the *profound transformations* going on in nations and make sure that the progress of science and technology does not recoil upon the spiritual development of peoples. The faithful form communities of their own but those communities, insofar as possible, should sink their roots in the culture of their nation.[17] In this connection Vatican II quotes from the Letter to Diognetus: Christians "are not marked off from other human beings by their native land, their language, or their way of behaving in civic life."[18] If the Church is to pursue its work of evangelization, it needs men and women who are especailly well trained.[19]

It is a fact that the great religious traditions have been producers of culture. In *Nostra Aetate* Vatican II alludes to "religions bound up with the progress of culture." It mentions, in particular, Hinduism, Buddhism, and other forms of religion that have tried "to anticipate the anxiety of the human heart by proposing ways—that is, teachings, rules of life, and sacred rites." Although differing with these religions on more than one point, the Church regards their teaching and ways of acting with sincere respect. It calls upon Christians to display prudence and love, and to engage in dialogue and collaboration with non-Christians. By bearing witness to their Christian faith, they participate in the cultural progress of those peoples. Christians must try to understand their cultures from within, "acknowledging, preserving, and promoting the spiritual, moral, and socio-cultural values that are found in them."[20]

Let me end this overview of Vatican II here. It clearly indicates that the official Church became profoundly sensitized at that council to socio-cultural realities and the new conditons surrounding its activity in the world. Our analysis of the relationship between the Church and culture will go deeper when we examine further on such specific problems as the evangelization of cultures, inculturation, and human cultural advancement. We shall then see even more clearly the light that Vatican II shed on the problems of our time.[21] Shifting to another approach right now, let me see how the Church came to modernize its perception of cultures. The next chapter will enable us to better appreciate the stages whereby the thinking of the Church gradually developed and matured insofar as its relationship with living cultures is concerned.

2/Church-Civilization-Culture: The Development of an Idea

As we saw in the preceding chapter, the Church at Vatican II clearly formulated its position vis-à-vis modern cultures. Culture became the privileged locus of Church activity, so to speak. We should realize, however, that the cultural orientation of the Church at Vatican II was the result of a slow and patient process of maturation. This end point presupposed progressive stages that had not always been easy. As *Gaudium et Spes* reminds us: "Although the Church has contributed much to the progress of culture, experience shows that, due to circumstantial reasons, it is not always easy to achieve harmony between culture and Christianity."[1]

To appreciate the full novelty and importance of the Vatican II position on the relationship between the Church and culture we must consider the stages whereby Christian perception was progressively enriched on this matter. The aim of this chapter is to examine the main documents of the Holy See from the time of Leo XIII to our own day and see how the view of the modern Church on the relationship between Christianity and cultures was gradually put together and spelled out.

It is worth mentioning that in an earlier day the documents of the Church spoke about "civilization," only rarely about "culture," except in the classic sense of the latter term. It is interesting to trace, in the terminology of successive popes, the notion of culture in the anthropological sense, a concept they use to analyse socio-cultural situations. This development was already perceptible with Pius XII, was made specific by John XXIII, and was solidly confirmed in the teachings of Paul VI and John Paul II. An examination of this evolution in Church documents will add further light to

14

the first chapter of this book which brought out the modernization of the Church's view of culture.

A look back at the statements of the popes will be particularly instructive, then, because it will help to bring out the extent to which the thinking of the Church has tried to respond to the diverse historical circumstances in which it has found itself.

THE CHURCH AS A TEACHER OF CIVILIZATION

In the days of Leo XIII it was natural to use the word "civilization," rather than the word "culture," to designate socio-historical realities. At the end of the nineteenth century the Church was openly accused of rejecting the "new civilization." It was subjected to the attacks of liberal agnosticism and illuminist or rationalist currents that openly depicted the Church as a retrograde force, an enemy of progress and civilization. In several of his official documents Leo XIII took pains to show that the Church, far from being an enemy of progress, had shown itself to be a great civilizing force throughout its history. In his first encyclical, *Inscrutabili* (1878), he reminds us that there could not be any real civilization without the foundation of eternal principles concerning truth, justice, and love, and without the help of immutable laws. The Church has effectively "promoted love of and the progress of the human sciences." The Church combatted superstitions, slavery, and barbarism. The Church salvaged pieces of ancient society and stopped it later from falling back into superstition. The Church "has everywhere civilized the human race in both its private and public morals." Why, then, is there attack on the Church, which has been a "teacher" and "mother" of civilization? "If the numerous benefits that we have just mentioned, which owe their origin to the ministry of the Church and its salutary influence, are truly the achievements and glories of human civilization, then it is false that the Church of Jesus Christ abhors and rejects civilization; for, as the Church sees it, to it belongs wholly the honor of having been the guardian, teacher, and mother of civilization."[2]

In his encyclical *Immortale Dei* (1885), dealing with the makeup of governments, Leo XIII draws an ideal portrait of what had once been the beneficial cooperation of the Church and governments: "There was a time when the philosophy of the gospel message governed states. In those days the sovereign force and influence of the Christian spirit penetrated the laws, institutions, popular customs, and organizations of states."[3] Religion constituted the grandeur and radiance of Europe, enabling it to "maintain preeminence in civilization."[4] To those who accuse the Church of harming the modern state Leo XIII replies by citing St. Augustine: "Try to find better citizens than those brought up in the doctrine of Christ; better soldiers, husbands, wives, sons, daughters, masters, servants, kings, magistrates, taxpayers, treasury officials—all of them imbued with the excellent quality required by Christian doctrine—and we shall see if they still can say that the Church is an obstacle to the well-being of the state."[5]

Benedict XV began his pontificate just after World War I, with its "colossal massacres," broke out. In his encyclical *Ad Beatissimi Apostolorum* (1914), dealing with the principles of charity and Christian justice, he patiently reminds all the belligerents of the root principle of charity taught by Christ and of "the basics of Christian philosophy." Before that, without using the expression, he speaks of a "civilization of love" and urges all Catholics, through their associations, their journals, and their efforts, to imbue all society with the principle of love of neighbor, which is based "on the gospel message as well as on human nature and both private and public interests." To be sure, love of neighbor cannot eliminate the differences between circumstances and social classes; but without charity there is a lapse into violence of all sorts. Catholics must be wary, above all, of succumbing to internal divisions that run directly counter to the teaching of the Church: "They should beware of certain appellations that have begun to circulate recently to differentiate Catholics from Catholics. . . . In its essentials Catholicism admits of neither more nor less. . . . Either one professes it in full or one does not profess it at all."[6]

CIVILIZATION, EDUCATION, AND THE SOCIAL QUESTION

With Pius XI the Church states its position more precisely, especially with respect to Christian education and the social question. In his encyclical *Divini Illius Magistri* (1929), dealing with the Christian education of the young, Pius XI championed the right of the Church in the domain of education and voiced its opposition to theories and political policies challenging that right at the time. Pursuing its vocation, the Church asserts its full right to be "the promoter of letters, sciences, and the arts . . . even establishing and maintaining its own schools and institutions in every field of learning and at every level of culture. This activity of the Church in every field of culture is of immense help to families and nations." Pius XI saw that the educational task of the Church extended even to nonbelievers, in the thousands of schools established by Christians in mission lands. There the Church continues its work, even as of old it inculcated the Christian way of life and civilization in "those peoples who today make up the various Christian nations of the civilized world." Voicing a challenge to those governments that dispute the Church's right and proper mission, Pius XI reechoes the argument of St. Augustine that had been used by Leo XIII.

Pius XI rebuts those who accuse Christian education of sidetracking citizens from important tasks in the earthly city, as if Christian principles of education were "opposed to societal life and material prosperity as well as to any and all progress in letters, the sciences, the arts, and other works of civilization." Appealing to the history of the Church, he cites the reply of Tertullian to his fellow citizens: "We are no strangers to life." As Tertullian explained the matter, Christians who honor God do not reject any earthly good. They use earthly things without going to excess, and they involve themselves in public life, commerce, and societal activities: "Like you, we plow the seas and fight wars, till the fields and engage in commerce, have business dealings with you and put our labors at your disposal. How can we seem useless for your affairs when we are immersed in them and live off them? I really do not see your point."[7] Thus, notes Pius XI, the Church as educator has manifested its civilizing capabilities throughout history: "This is demonstrated by the whole history of Christianity and its institutions. It has been identified with the history of true civilization and progress right down to our own day." Spreading the ideal of holiness, the Church has been present and active in every sector of society and among all classes, professions, and states of life: "from the simple, rural peasant to the learned scholar; from the private man who is the father of a family to the king who rules peoples and nations; from peasant girls and housewives to queens and empresses." Over and over again in *Divini Illius Magistri*, Pius XI underlines the civilizing role of the Church as it goes about its evangelizing mission.

In his social teaching, too, Pius XI came back to the theme of Christian civilization. In *Quadragesimo Anno* (1931), for example, he notes that the principles of the Church on social matters have spread far and wide in the world in the forty years since Leo XIII issued his great encyclical on the social order, *Rerum Novarum*. That is mark of real progress for the Church: "Catholic principles on social matters have gradually become the common heritage of humanity." The progress of the Church's social doctrine is now visible in the press, the parliaments, and courts. It is clear to Pius XI that the Church's social teaching is now the main way for the Church to pass along Christian values to contemporary societies and cultures. Pius XI analyzes the changes that have taken place in the capitalist system and various branches of socialism, and he also points up the fundamental principles underlying the establishment of a just and harmonious society. With regard to the social teaching of the Church, he calls for a twofold reform, that of institutions and that of morals, and he reiterates what Leo XIII had said: "If human society is to be healed, it will be healed only through a return to the life and institutions of Christianity."[8]

Pius XI was especially preoccupied with the rise of various forms of totalitarianism, and with atheistic communism above all. His encyclical *Divini Redemptoris* (1937) begins with a consideration of "Christian civilization". Fulfilling human hopes, the Savior of the world came to earth and "inaugurated a new universal civilization, Christian civilization, immensely superior to what humanity had laboriously achieved in a few privileged nations."[9] Now, alas, that civilization is in danger, menaced by a new barbarism: "Entire peoples are in danger of lapsing into a barbarism worse than that in which most of the world found itself at the coming of the Redeemer."[10] Liberalism itself had smoothed the way for communism. Christians must find the principles of discernment needed to confront it. All believers are urged to draw inspiration from the social doctrine of the Church and engage in joint action against atheistic materialism. For its part, the Church is striving to inculcate "the means whereby Christian civilization, the only *civitas* that is truly *humana*, can be saved."[11]

CHRISTIAN CIVILIZATION AND SOCIAL RECONSTRUCTION

With Pius XII the idea of Christian civilization took on particular importance. He returned to it frequently, adding points and specifics required by the circumstances in which the Church was then living. It was toward the end of World War II, in particular, that he chose to deal specifically with the subject in a radio message devoted to "the function of Christian civilization."[12]

At that point in time, an international conference on the reorganization of the postwar world was taking place at Dunbarton Oaks in Washington, D.C. Faced with a world in ruins, Pius XII appealed to the human conscience, and to the Christian conscience above all. On the response to that appeal, he said, "depends the fate of Christian civilization in Europe and throughout the world." Far from resenting the different forms of civil communities, Christian civilization reinforces them by grounding them on moral law and respect for the human person: "Rather than enfeebling or suffocating the sound elements of diverse national cultures, Christian civilization harmonizes their essential elements and thus creates a broad unity of sentiments and moral norms. This is the solid foundation for true peace, social justice, and fraternal love among the members of the great human family."

Pius XII draws attention to a paradox. On the one hand, Christian civilization seems undermined from its very foundations; on the other, it seems to be spreading more and more. "Some have come to forget this precious patrimony, to neglect or even repudiate it. But the fact of this hereditary succession remains." Its voice continues to make itself heard as "the echo of this Christian heritage."

Aware of the extreme gravity of the moment, Pius XII issued an urgent appeal that the patrimony of Christian civilization be saved "above and beyond any and all collaboration with divergent ideological or social tendencies, sometimes suggested by purely contingent motives." And he stated the reason: "Fidelity to the heritage of Christian civilization and vigorous defense of it against anti-Christian and atheistic currents are the keystone that can never be sacrificed for the sake of a temporary advantage or bargain." Pius XII was confident that his appeal would have "a favorable echo among millions of human spirits on earth," and would be able to inspire loyal and effective collaboration in the framing of a new juridical order, an element which appears to be "especially required by Christian thought." Pius XII had no doubt that Christian civilization would be the foundation of the society of the future, a society built upon peace, justice, and mutual love among human beings. There was nothing authoritarian in Pius XII's assertion. There was nothing unrealistic about proposing the evangelical values of justice and charity as principles for societal renewal.

A few months later, Pius XII returned to this question when he spoke about "the future of democracy." He takes delight in the thought that "the time is past when persons might have believed that calling humanity back to moral and evangelical principles was to be disdainfully ruled out as something unrealistic for the life of governments and peoples."[13] In this Christmas radio message, and especially in his radio message quoted earlier, Pius XII injects an important specification for any correct understanding of the notion of "Christian civilization."

It would be incorrect to think that the Church is proposing some system of spiritual domination of the whole world. Pius XII spells out what is meant by "Christian civilization," which is essentially grounded on *the social teaching of the Church*. In his radio message of September 1944, devoted specifically to "Christian civilization," he reserves the whole second part for *economic and social questions*, viewed in the light of Christian thought: the dignity of the human person, the rights and duties of ownership, a critique of capitalism, the rights and duties of public organisms, the duty of Catholics to dedicate themselves to the promotion of social justice, and so forth.

He spells out his thinking even more clearly at the end of World War II, in an address on the role of the Church in the reconstruction of human society (Feb. 20, 1946). Once again he notes that the role of the Church is not comparable to that of an immense empire. The Church essentially acts *within the heart of the human being*. The Church's moral authority is not exercised as the authority of an earthly power might be: "It is not the function of the Church to envelop and somehow embrace all of human society as an immense global empire might. This concept of the Church as an earthly empire with world dominion is fundamentally false." In no period of history, says Pius XII, has this conception corresponded to reality, because the Church proceeds in the opposite way: "The Church's progress and expansion take the opposite route from that of modern imperialism." The Church seeks first the human being and its spiritual progress.

Pius XII describes the ideal citizen formed by the Church, "which rears human beings to the perfection of their being and vitality in order to give human society persons so formed." He enumerates four essential elements: the inviolable integrity of the human being created in the image of God; human beings proud of their dignity and liberty; human beings rightly jealous of their common equality in all that has to do with human dignity; and human beings attached to their land and traditions. Herein lies the nature of the Church's spiritual power and authority: "This, then, is the real meaning and practical influence of the supranationality of the Church. . . . The Church rises above all differences, all times, and all places, and thereby unceasingly builds on the solid foundation of any and every human society."

CHRISTIAN CULTURE AND ISSUES OF JUSTICE AND PEACE

The theme of culture and its relationships to the Church was equally frequent in the messages of John XXIII. He placed particular stress on the links between culture and justice, and I shall return to that subject in chapter 4. In the teaching of John XXIII we see gradually taking shape the major ideas that will be affirmed in the documents of Vatican II, and particularly in *Gaudium et Spes*. For the moment it is enough to point out that two of his encyclicals, *Mater et Magistra* (1961) and *Pacem in Terris* (1963), did a great deal to broadcast Christian social doctrine far and wide; they attracted the attention of specialists, social movements, governments, and international organizations. In the eyes of John XXIII, the Church's social thought is not destined for Catholics alone. The pope speaks for the whole world, and John XXIII wanted to bear testimony to that fact by addressing his encyclical on peace, *Pacem in Terris*, not only to episcopates and Catholics but also to "all human beings of good will," as he writes in his preamble. It should be noted that in both *Mater et Magistra* and *Pacem in Terris* Catholics are urged to work even with persons who hold a different conception of life or who profess no religion, so long as certain preconditions are respected, which have to do especially with religion, morality, and the rights of ecclesiastical authority. Catholics are given the directive: "Let them be animated by a spirit of understanding and disinterestedness, and ready to cooperate loyally in matters that are good in themselves or can be turned to good."[14]

In *Pacem in Terris* John XXIII calls upon Catholics to distinguish always between "error itself and those who commit it." "The person who has strayed into error still remains a human being and retains his or her dignity as a person, which must always be given due consideration."[15] The pope likewise urges Catholics to distinguish between *doctrines* and *social movements*. We should not equate "erroneous philosophical doctrines on the nature, origin, and destiny of the universe and of the human being with historical movements that have a socio-economic or cultural aim, even if those movements owe their origin to, and still draw their inspiration from, those theoretical doctrines." In accordance with the norms of prudence, it is legitimate to recognize in such movements elements that are "positive and worthy of approval." The norms of prudence, the social teaching of the Church, and the directives of ecclesiastical authority should make it possible for Catholics to decide whether it is the right moment for collaboration with non-

Catholics and "the manner and extent of such cooperation on social, economic, cultural, or political matters, for useful purposes and the true welfare of the community."[16]

The pope's observations are objectively important and would merit extended treatment. The important point to stress here is the growing consciousness that the Church must operate from now on in *pluralistic cultures*. Defending the human being should be the common objective of all honest persons of good will, whatever their spiritual convictions. Promoting the cause of human dignity should awaken in the whole world a new sense of shared responsibility and cooperation. Christians should be the first to promote this "civilization of universal solidarity," an idea that would be particularly dear to Paul VI and John Paul II. In the eyes of history John XXIII is the pope who envisioned and convened Vatican II. Perhaps even more than his writings, his prophetic act was, in germinal form, the updating or aggiornamento of the Church in today's culture. Vatican II would demonstrate the full fruitfulness of his daring, providential decision.

To conclude this chapter, I shall consider how the major guidelines of Vatican II with respect to culture have inspired the thinking and action of the popes who undertook the mission of implementing Vatican II.

THE POPES OF MODERN CULTURE

It is very significant to hear Paul VI and John Paul II using the language of cultural analysis and action readily and easily.

The topic of civilization and culture was especially dear to Paul VI, and he never ceased to deal with it in his oral addresses and writings. His famous encyclical *Populorum Progressio* (1967), which could be regarded as an encyclical on the culture of human progress, was viewed by some as a major event in civilization. Right after its publication the economist François Perroux said: "It is one of the greatest texts of human history. It radiates a kind of rational, moral, and religious testimony."[17]

Another major document of Paul VI was *Evangelii Nuntiandi* (1975), which is practically the charter dealing with the evangelization of cultures. I shall return to it later. Right now the point to note is that Paul VI was the first pope to use the terminology of cultural sociology in the modern sense. His basic contribution will be examined later, but let me dwell for a moment on the beautiful expression he coined and introduced into the idiom of the church: the "civilization of love."

The first mention of "a civilization of love" was made by Paul VI on Pentecost Day of 1970. Addressing the crowd from his balcony, the Pope spoke to them in the following terms: "It is a civilization of love and peace that Pentecost inaugurated, and we all know how much today the world is in need of love and peace." This beautiful expression was to be constantly taken up and repeated again and again. At the close of the Jubilee Year of 1975, Paul VI stressed the rich significance of the expression, indicating how the civilization of love would have to be the crowning point of the Holy Year.

How can one explain the success of this expression if not by the fact that Paul VI was able to make himself the faithful interpreter of the aspirations of his contemporaries. Our world is tired of strife, violence, terrorism, and war; perhaps never in all of history has there been such deeply felt universal desire for peace and solidarity.

In his very first encyclical *Ecclesian Sanctam* (1964), Paul VI sent out a pressing appeal for understanding in today's world and for fraternal dialogue with all Christians, all believers, and all men and women of good will.

It is out of a sense of love inspired by the Gospel that the Church, by practicing a kind of cultural communion—by adopting this "primary universality"—embraces in the fullest sense of the word the cause of humanity. An immense affection for humankind as such manifests itself in the pope's words.

At the opening of the second session of Vatican II in 1963, Pope Paul VI made himself an advocate of universal charity. He called the Church to a reaffirmation of its identity and to a spiritual reawakening, generously proposing "an ecumenicity which is nothing less than total and universal and the construction of a bridge to the contemporary world." In deeply moving words, he spoke of the Church's radical love for humanity: "The Church's missionary vocation, that is to say, her essential vocation, is to make humanity, in whatever condition it happens to be, the fond object of its evangelical mission."

This message of love for modern men and women was emphasized in an unforgettable manner in the Pope's discourse at the close of the Vatican II. "At the close of the Council," he said, "an outpouring of affection and admiration stretches out over the whole modern world. Let us condemn error wherever it exists, but let such an action be taken only because both charity and truth demand it, and our action is but an echo of true respect and love. Rather than offering disheartening diagnoses, the Council offers hopeful remedies; rather than catastrophic forecasts, the Council offers words of hope. The Council has thus not only respected but honored the values of the contemporary world, sustained its efforts, and purified and consecrated its aspirations." Paul VI thus did not conceal the fragile nature of modern humanity and its miseries but, above all, he wished to proclaim the love of the Church for every brother and sister. The Pope uses moving words to make clear that it is the love for our fellowmen that makes us recognize the face of Christ: "It is in the face of every individual rendered particularly transparent through the tears and pain that we can and must recognize the face of Christ" (7 December, 1965).

For Paul VI, only in love does human civilization find the foundation of its harmony. This message is evident in the encyclical *Humanae Vitae* (1968). There the Pope exalts the love which proceeds from God as the dynamic principle of the family, of social order and of all of civilization: "Conjugal love reveals its true nature and nobility when it is considered in its supreme Source, in the God who is Love . . . Marriage, then, is not a haphazard effect or the result of an unconscious evolution of natural forces but is a wise institution of the Creator for realizing in humanity his design of love" (no.8). The Pope specified that "the Church knows that it contributes to the establishment of a truly human civilization by defending conjugal morality in its integrity" (no.18).

We can say that "the civilization of love" represents one of Paul VI's richest pastoral statements. To work efficaciously toward the construction of such a civilization, various conditions will be required. 1) First of all, it will be necessary to consider culture as a specific area for evangelization, namely the spirit of Christ must penetrate attitudes and behavior. 2) To establish a civilization of love will similarly demand for Christians a new type of evangelization, which will render the message of Christ's love credible and attractive to modern cultures. It is necessary to act at the level of the individual and at the same time at the level of cultural realities as such—dealing at the same time also with common attitudes, models of behavior, collective values, orientations of the media, and the like. Paul VI said in his *Evangelii Nuntiandi* (no.18) that the Church "seeks to convert the personal as well as the collective conscience of humanity." 3) The action of the Church will extend also to cooperation with everyone of good will in defense and promotion of human dignity, of justice, and of the integral culture of all. 4) This undertaking presupposes an engagement with culture in its popular and anthropological aspects as well as in its humanistic, intellectual, aesthetic, and scientific sense. 5) To propose a civilization of love demands, in short, a veritable act of faith in the future of society, a confidence in the human capacity to build a form of common life together able to bring about the original brotherhood of man.[18]

Paul VI proposed for our times something more than a utopia; his idea of building a civilization of love continues to stimulate Christians, who in their respect for liberty offer for our times a truly generous ideal for the future of culture. John Paul II has constantly reaffirmed the validity and actuality of this message. He declared to the Pontifical Council for Culture in 1985 that "the Church respects all cultures and does not impose her faith in Jesus Christ on anyone, but invites all of good will to promote a true civilization of love founded on the Gospel of brotherly love, justice, and dignity for all."

The closest collaborators of Paul VI tell us that he had actually considered creating an organism of the Holy See for the evangelization of culture. The idea, however, did not find concrete expression until 1982, at the beginning of John Paul II's papacy, when, after thorough consultation, he decided to found the Pontifical Council for Culture.

With John Paul II the theologico-cultural perspective of Vatican II has been enriched and deepened, so much so that *culture* seems to be one of the major poles of his pontificate. For him the *Church's dialogue with cultures* in our day is of capital importance for the future of the Church and the world. Addressing the cardinals, called to Rome for a special meeting on November 5, 1979, John Paul II stated: "You are certainly aware of the extent to which I, both personally and through my collaborators, intend to devote myself to the problems of culture, science, and the arts. It is a vital domain, on which the fate of the Church and the world depends as we come to the end of this century."[19]

John Paul II drew the practical consequences of this view and envisaged creating an organism that would give new impetus to the whole Church in its dialogue with cultures. Recognizing and appreciating the cultural and educational work already being done by the Holy See,[20] he foresaw the creation of a Vatican organism that would further heighten the Church's involvement with culture and cultures.

In May 1982 John Paul II proceeded to create the Pontifical Council for Culture (PCC), in order to give the whole Church "a common impetus" in the encounter of the gospel message with the plurality of cultures. This Council would bear witness to the interest of the Holy See in cultures. In its own proper way it would try to better harmonize the work of Catholics in the cultural realm, to ensure a more pointed presence of the Church in international organisms and congresses, and to follow more closely the cultural policy of governments. The main aims assigned to the Council for Culture can be summed up as follows:

1. to bear witness to the Holy See's profound interest in the progress of culture and in dialogue between cultures and the Church;

2. to take part in the cultural activities of Vatican organisms and the cultural institutions of the Holy See so as to improve coordination;

3. to establish a dialogue with the episcopal conferences so as to encourage a beneficial sharing of cultural research, initiative, and action undertaken by local Churches and to pass these benefits along to the entire Church;

4. to work with international Catholic organizations (academic, historical, philosophical, theological, scientific, artistic, and intellectual) and promote cooperation among them;

5. to follow, in its own proper way, the cultural work of UNESCO, the Council of Europe, and other organizations involved in the betterment of humanity;

6. to ensure the effective presence of the Holy See at international congresses dealing with the sciences, culture, and education;

7. to be concerned with the cultural policy and activity of governments around the world;

8. to facilitate cultural dialogue between the Church and universities, as well as organizations of artists, specialists, researchers, and scholars, and to promote meaningful encounters in these cultural realms;

9. to welcome personalities from the world of culture who wish to become more familiar with the Church's cultural activity and to give the Holy See the benefits of their experience.

The role assigned to the Pontifical Council for Culture illustrates the approach that the Church intends to follow in its dialogue with cultures. Obviously, the PCC could not operate in an authoritarian way. The Church's action in this area does not involve commanding cultures but rather being present to them as a leaven. The modus operandi, then, will entail listening, meeting, research, dialogue, presence rooted in understanding, and discernment. This work presupposes ongoing collaboration, not only among Catholics, but also with all believers and all persons of good will. Culture is a common ground where all those interested in the future and development of humanity can meet for joint action. "This Council will pursue its own specific aims in an ecumenical and fraternal spirit, promoting dialogue with non-Christian religions and with persons or groups who hold to no religion, in joint pursuit of cultural communication with all human beings of good will."[21]

Two guiding and complementary tasks are specified for the PCC, and these directives hold true for the Church as a whole in its encounter with cultures: *the evangelization of cultures* and *the defense of humankind in its culture.*

Thus the action of John Paul II crowns a long process of patient growth and maturation in the Church, from the time of Leo XIII onward. In their own way all of them have tried to involve the Holy See in the encounter with cultures and the promotion of humankind. John Paul II has stressed that these two tasks are urgent and crucial both for Christians and for the whole human family:

> More than once I have chosen to point out that today the Church's dialogue with cultures is of vital importance for the future of the Church and the world. Permit me to return to the matter and stress *two major and complementary aspects* that correspond to the two levels of the Church's activity in this area: *the evangelization of cultures* and *the defense of humankind and its cultural betterment.* Both of these tasks require us to spell out clearly new approaches for the Church's dialogue with the cultures of our time.[22]

It is in the very heart of this cultural reality that the Church now defines its evangelizing work. It seeks to better understand the linkages between faith and cultures, showing how the gospel message can become a cultural leaven. All this presupposes a *new perception of the reality of culture* on the part of Christians and an inducement to have an impact on living culture by finding inspiration in the principles of theology and help in the human sciences.

The remarkable thing, which marks a real development in the thinking of the Church, is the fact that it has given front and center stage in social discourse to the concrete, historical human being, today's human being, creative and full of hope but also tragically fragile and menaced. The Church has resolutely turned to modernity and thus bears credible witness in our time to its unconditional love for the human being.

The Church is a promoter of the *humanum*, and it has outlined the two basic approaches involved in the cultural work of Christians. First, on a more elementary level, the task is to defend humankind and its culture for the simple reason that humankind has been created in the image of God. On a higher level, the Church intends to pursue, in freedom, the fruitful encounter of cultures with the gospel message. These two objectives will be examined in part 2 and part 3 of this book. Part 4 will deal with the activity of the Church insofar as it relates to culture understood as the sciences and the arts. This latter activity, too, is closely connected with the two objectives noted above.

PART TWO

DEFENSE OF THE HUMAN BEING AND HUMAN CULTURE

Modern humanity is confronted with a curious paradox. On the one hand, it has managed to create technological marvels unknown to any previous civilization. On the other hand, it feels threatened as never before by the products of its mind and spirit. Today every man and woman is wondering what the future holds for the human being, who is threatened by atomic conflagration, ecological devastation, biological upsets, and various forms of ideological domination. The major thing at stake in technological society is primarily cultural in nature.

Only an ethical surge and a mobilization of the world's conscience will be able to defend humanity. Inspired by a radical love for the human being, the Church is coming to the *defense of culture*, the sole assurance of survival and progress (chap. 3).

We now grasp more clearly that if we are to promote human development, we must simultaneously heed the imperatives of justice and those of culture. The primary needs of the human being are both physical and cultural at the same time. *Culture, justice,* and *peace* are necessarily intertwined objectives (chap. 4).

On the political level, these principles call for new commitments on the part of governments. The modern nations are translating these exigencies into *cultural policies*; the latter must find their inspiration in an ethical aim that respects the cultural rights of all citizens (chap. 5).

3/Defense of Human Culture

Since the not so distant day when André Malraux was worried about the "precarious human being," the condition of the human being has steadily deteriorated. We need only look at the facts around us: the rise of fanaticisms and racisms, growing terrorism and criminality, interminable wars, the insane arms race, and the poverty and underdevelopment that bring humiliation to an ever-increasing portion of humanity. The most serious thing may well be the crumbling of human *reasons for living*, both those of individual persons and those of whole cultures.

Such is the tragic paradox of an age that proclaims, as never before, the rights of the human being and its development on the one hand, yet continues to totally disregard its most elementary dignity on the other. Millions of oppressed and starving human beings bear witness to this fact in dramatic silence, a silence that will become explosive.

But there is a *sign of hope*, I think. These calamities that haunt us all have now become part of our collective anguish, and they project before us the image of the human being threatened in its very humanity, in what makes it human, *its culture*. We all have been brought face to face with our responsibilities, and that could be beneficial. But the defense of the human being will be a very demanding task.

Is humanity threatened more by famine, nuclear apocalypse, or the ongoing disintegration of human cultures? At bottom, there is only one peril, dehumanization, which can lead just as easily to biological annihilation as to the death of the human spirit. There lies the last line of defense for the human being.

31

THE PRECARIOUS HUMAN BEING

Given the extent of the danger, moral denunciation is necessary; but it is not enough. The problem is no longer merely ethical. It has become an *ontological* problem because *the human being* and its future are at stake. For us, then, the defense of the human being's culture has to do with a radical issue: the very survival of the *humanum*. So let us take a realistic look at the grave threats that loom over our future, but let us also note the signs of hope that presage a new awareness of the collective stakes involved and the challenge that must be met.

THREATENED AS NEVER BEFORE

Since Vatican II the Church has stepped forward in an increasingly visible way as the advocate of the human being, and it has moved to the defense of humankind as such. The reason is that never before in history has humankind been so serious threatened in terms of its being and its reasons for living. This is the great drama of our time, and John Paul II gave a good description of this sad paradox of our age:

> Perhaps one of the most glaring weaknesses of present-day civilization lies in an inadequate view of humankind. Undoubtedly our age is the age that has written and spoken the most about humankind; it is the age of various humanisms, the age of anthropocentrism. But paradoxically it is also the age of humankind's deepest anxieties about its identity and destiny; it is the age when human beings have been debased to previously unheard-of levels, when human values have been trodden underfoot as never before.[1]

The human race has wondrously extended its ability to dominate the universe, but this power threatens to slip from its control and turn against it. Its mastery over creation is accompanied by a *moral and cultural misery* that menaces its future. The Church's task is essentially one of evangelization. But the Church realizes that in the name of its own proper vocation it must also defend the human being and its culture, prompted by what may be called a radical love for humankind.

What is it that menaces humanity at this point? It is primarily what humanity fabricates or produces by means of its technology, its intelligence, its ideologies, its selfish calculations, and its collective projects. The *productions* of human beings are in danger of turning completely against them: "The fear is that they could become the means and instruments of an unimaginable self-destruction eclipsing all the known cataclysms and catastrophes of human history."[2]

The future of humanity is riddled with anxiety. Human beings have invented the nuclear fire that threatens to destroy every trace of civilization. They can also provoke an ecological crisis that would jeopardize the preconditions for life on earth. They are undertaking genetic experiments that theaten to shatter the biological equilibrium of humankind. In the cultural, ideological, and philosophical realms, the threats are different but no less formidable. For more than a generation we have seen the propagation of theories that *demoralize* the human being in the literal sense of that word. In the minds of some, and of the young in particular, they have destroyed the conviction that humans are free, responsible beings capable of managing their moral conduct, knowing the absolute, and transcending themselves.

Human beings are also at the mercy of all forms of exploitation and manipulation, motivated by egotistical interests or dehumanizing ideologies. All these situations generate anxiety and deep unrest for the human family as a whole. Humanity is seriously menaced by *anticulture*.

It is the very humanity of human beings that is in danger of deteriorating. John Paul II has drawn a very realistic picture of the human condition in this century: "Up to now it has been a century of major disasters for humanity, a century of terrible devastations, not only material but also and perhaps mainly moral. . . . A century when human beings have prepared a great deal of injustice and suffering for themselves."[3]

MORAL MISERY AND CULTURAL MISERY

Our contemporaries have actually inflicted upon themselves a situation of moral and cultural misery with astonishingly perverse effects. Injustice, totalitarian oppression of entire peoples, moral permissiveness, and spiritual degradation are certainly not new or specific to our age. But what strikes the observer is the fact that in a relatively brief span of time humanity has had to confront new problems, unheard of by virtue of their seriousness and the dramatic fact that they threaten fundamental values and the very survival of the human race. A few examples seem to be symptomatic.

In the name of rightist or leftist ideologies, totalitarian systems maintain whole populations in a condition of interior exile. Concentration-camp regimes are imposed on the masses for reasons of state. They do not hesitate to turn thousands of real or alleged opponents into the "disappeared." Torture is practiced systematically, its victims being thousands of defendants, suspects, or persons who are simply political opponents. Psychiatric imprisonment has become an ordinary means to restore persons to "normalcy" *or* to intimidate dissidents. We note the contagion of terrorism, conceived as a means of political destabilization or as an instrument of revolutionary anarchy. Another anticultural phenomenon is extremely troubling: the spread of drugs and their ravages. They are particularly evident among young persons in the affluent countries, but the plague is also reaching the Third World. And we cannot help but notice that the power and ramifications of this system of exploitation seem to defy civilized societies.

These realities are serious in themselves, of course; but they are especially serious because they signify a *contempt for the human being as such*. One does not hesitate to destroy persons physically or psychologically. Innocents are massacred, whole populations are systematically terrorized. For a growing number of individuals and systems, the human being counts for nothing. As I noted above, the threat is ontological because the *being* of the human person is in danger of being destroyed. There is certainly a need for moral denunciation, but that will remain ineffectual if it does not spur a defense of the *human being* as such. The fight for culture lies on that level now and in the future. That is the essential point to be gleaned from the above observations.

Some other facts can be cited that bear witness to the present trend toward *anticulture* and antihumanism. Moral permissiveness is not only a fact but a principle of action. It is legitimized and justified by new psychological theories; but it, too, is an attack on the human being, who must assume responsibility for its own acts. The generalization of abortion legislation in many countries and the tranquil spread of euthanasia are also facts that are relatively new and typical of an age dramatically surrendering basic respect for the human being.

In vast areas of the world we find a generalized state of underdevelopment. It is often due to situations of deliberate injustice that have created infrahuman and intolerable conditions for millions of men and women. To be sure, underdevelopment cannot always be directly attributed to deliberate crimes or injustices; but to the extent that these situations of poverty and misery are tolerated, they do become counts of indictment. How much more culpable, then, are those who directly or indirectly provoke such situations of suffering, servitude, and degradation.

Around us we find systems of exploitation or oppression that presuppose, at least tacitly, contempt for the human being. I am thinking of seriously restrictive demographic policies that are imposed on poor countries as preconditions for technical, military, or economic assistance. I am also thinking of price policies for imports or exports that seek only the enrichment of their makers or those who benefit from them, especially the big national and multinational corporations. The very fact of conceiving economic and political relations between nations in such terms constitutes *contempt for the human being itself*. It will not do to say that such a conception abstracts from that issues. The very fact that the human being is not taken into account is to be condemned on moral grounds.

Let me add here the very serious matter of the arms race, on which not only affluent countries but also those of the Third World are squandering incalculable sums of money and other resources. So much the less is thus available for the betterment of the human family. Here again we find a reversal that is antihuman and inadmissible.

In all these examples the victim is the *human being* itself, who is treated with contempt and whose dignity and elementary needs are trodden underfoot. Note that the effect, dehumanization, touches the perpetrators of injustice and oppression as well as their victims, though obviously in opposite ways. For our purposes here we may draw this basic conclusion: few ages in history have so radically imperiled the human being, its dignity, and its culture.

THE CULTURAL DEGRADATION OF ADVANCED SOCIETIES

The most technologically advanced societies may well be those that run the greatest risk, because in them we see a profound deterioration of basic respect for the person, its dignity, its liberty, or its bedrock culture. Liberty is too often equated with amoral individualism, with the cravings of instinct or self-interest. Progress is equated with material enrichment or the accumulation of profit. Happiness is equated with a culture of indiscriminate consumption. The primacy of subjectivity is heightened by the prevailing hedonism, the immediate gratification of desires, the worship of comfort, and the refusal of definitive commitment. Human beings in these countries often seem to have despaired of their own humanity and to be prisoners of their own false needs. The most affluent societies are suffering a *crisis of the human being*. As John Paul II put it: "These societies are facing the crisis of the human being specifically. It entails a growing lack of confidence in their own humanity, in what it means to be a human being, and a consequent lack of affirmation and joy that should follow from that awareness and be a source of creativity. Contemporary civilization is trying to impose on the human being a series of specious imperatives."[4] The future of humanity is threatened when it renounces its culture, as John Paul II points out: "All that indirectly expresses a terrible and systematic renunciation of the healthy ambition . . . to be human."[5]

The basic problem facing present-day humanity is the necessity of *harmonizing its achievements*. This means its scientific and technical achievements on the one hand, which have produced marvels never known before, and its spiritual and ethical achievements on the other hand, which are the apex of human creativity. Consider everything that our contemporaries admire as achievements of our civilization. Do they make human beings more human, more aware of their dignity, more responsible, more open to others?

If culture is the thing whereby the human being becomes more human, then it must be said that our age is threatened by *anticulture*: threatened by the dehumanization and desacralization of the human being. The capabilities of the human being have turned their power against the welfare of the human being. Speaking to men and women of culture in Korea, John Paul II drew a gripping portrait of the "precarious human being":

> Due to a lack of wisdom in the use of human capabilities, biological human existence is menaced by irreparable pollution, genetic manipulation, and the suppression of unborn lives. Its moral being is in danger of becoming a prey to nihilistic hedonism, indiscriminate consumption, the erosion of all sense of values and, in our day to a degree never known before, unjust systems that exploit whole populations. Political and ideological programs are oppressing the deeper soul of whole populations. As a result, they are forced into a uniform apathy or an attitude of complete mistrust of others.[6]

Awareness of the threats that now face the human family is spreading to all. Today billions of men and women are living in continual fear of the future.

Undoubtedly, the most crucial factor in this moral awakening was the tragedy of Hiroshima. There, for the first time, humanity realized to its astonishment that it could destroy itself completely with the dreadful product of its technology. John Paul II expressed this with deep emotion when he addressed representatives of science and culture in Hiroshima on February 25, 1981.[7] Few events in history have reverberated so loudly in the human conscience as did the explosions of Hiroshima and Nagasaki. We all came to realize that humanity could destroy itself and all the achievements of civilization. The future, then, calls for a moral leap on the part of the whole human family. It is precisely in this context that the Church cries out to our contemporaries: *we must save the human being*, and this can be done only by loving humankind for itself. This is the message of elementary charity that the church voices to a humanity in danger of degradation and self-destruction.

HOPES FOR THE FUTURE OF CULTURE

UNCONDITIONAL LOVE FOR THE HUMAN BEING

It is both a sign of the times and a hope: a new awareness of the human problem is surfacing in the world. We shall find many different proofs of this in the following pages. Consider, for a moment, that today the Church appears before world opinion as one of the most loyal advocates of the human being and its culture. The fact is that the modern Church has taken upon itself completely these anxieties and uncertainties about the future of human beings and the survival of humanity. This solicitude is inspired by an unconditional love for the human being, who has been created in the image of God and possesses a unique dignity and grandeur in the universe. The Church loves and defends the human being for its own sake, for no other reason or pretext. Some might think that the Church, in so doing, is displaying a humanism that is hard to reconcile with its evangelizing vocation. Is not the Church mainly interested in humanity in order to evangelize, convert, and baptize it? Of course, the Church wants to teach the Good News to all nations and all human beings. But it also gives testimony of a radical, primary love for the human being itself as it is: that is, in its concrete existence with all its hopes, anxieties, and needs.

Christian history offers abundant illustrations of this solicitude for human beings, especially for the oppressed, the poor, the sick,

who deserve full attention and devotion whatever their response
to the gospel message may be. The poor and the sick are not asked
to undergo conversion before they are cared for and healed,
because the human being, in and of itself, deserves love and
esteem whatever its condition may be. John Paul II reaffirmed this
point before UNESCO in a tone of deep affection: "We must *affirm
the human being for its own sake,* and not for any other motive or
reason. . . . Indeed, we must love the human being because it is a
human being; we must demand love for the human being by
reason of the particular dignity the human being possesses."[8]

Now *defense of the human being* is, first of all, defense of that
which makes one human. It is defense of the human being's
culture, of its moral responsibility: "The most important thing is
always *the human being,* the human being and *its moral authority,* the
latter deriving from the truth of its principles and the conformity of
its acts with those principles."[9] To appreciate the meaning of this
urgent appeal, we must move beyond a simplistic moralism that
would view the Church solely as a moral authority engaged in
judging and condemning. The issues at stake go infinitely deeper.
What must be saved here is the ethical sense itself and the ontological reality of the moral conscience. The future of humanity
depends completely on our real and effective ability to set forth
ethical choices on both the individual and the collective level.

After the tragedy of Hiroshima this fact has progressively forced
itself on the human conscience worldwide. It is only by our
collective moral choices that we shall save humanity. In the past it
was possible to destroy a city or a country; now the whole planet is
threatened. We all are faced with a basic moral option: "Henceforth humanity can survive only by a conscious choice and an
elaborated politics. The moral and political choice confronting us is
that of putting all our resources of spirit, science, and culture in the
service of peace and the building of a new society."[10] One can now
say that defending the primacy of ethics means ensuring survival
of the human being, its dignity, and its basic culture.

MOBILIZATION OF EVERY HUMAN CONSCIENCE

The scope of the challenge prompts the Church to encourage a
mobilization of every human conscience: "We must mobilize consciences. We must augment the efforts of human consciences to
match the tension between good and evil that weighs upon human
beings as the twentieth century draws to a close. They must be

convinced of the priority of ethics over technology, of the primacy of the person over things, of the superiority of spirit over matter." Making this appeal to UNESCO, John Paul II struck a note of urgency because the threat weighs upon all.

The Church addresses its appeal to all upright, sincere human beings, to all those who believe in the values of the spirit; and it urges them to love the human being for itself, whatever their beliefs may be. There is an urgent need to mobilize the world's conscience, to reawaken the sense of the human in all.

The cause of the human being and its culture is a privileged place of *encounter* and *collaboration* for all persons of good will. Christians are called to an effort at careful discernment, so that they may pinpoint all those persons who are faithfully trying to serve humanity: "You will find that the spirit of goodness is mysteriously at work in many of our contemporaries, even in those who claim no religion but who are honestly trying to fulfill their human vocation in a courageous way."[11]

Billions of men and women today are experiencing these yearnings for an integral development of the human, which presupposes a mobilization of minds and consciences. A conversion of a cultural nature, then, is needed to save the human being as such, who will continue to exist only in and through its culture. That is why John Paul II ended his address to UNESCO with this bold assertion: "Yes, the future of humanity depends on culture. Yes, the peace of the world depends on the primacy of the spirit. Yes, the peaceful future of humanity depends on love."[12]

EDUCATION AS THE FIRST TASK OF CULTURE

Defending the culture of the human being ultimately comes down to promoting its dignity, liberty, and sense of responsibility. This cultural objective can be achieved primarily by *education*, by the moral and intellectual sensitization of the greatest number. Education and culture are inseparable: "The first and essential task of culture in general, and of all culture as well, is education. Education comes down to this: that the human being becomes ever more human; that it can *be* more and not just *have* more; and that, as a result, it is wise enough to become ever more fully human through all that it has and possesses."[13] Let me quickly indicate here the conditions and exigencies of a cultural education, given that I shall return to this matter in later chapters.

We must first underline the necessary link that should exist between education, culture, and family milieu. It is in the family that the child learns its native language, the primary vehicle of all culture. It is in the family that the child is molded to social life, mutual interchange, and a sense of moral responsibility, dedication, and solidarity. The family, then, must be viewed as the basic creative milieu of culture.[14]

To defend the human being today is also to uphold *its essential rights* as they find expression in such documents as the Universal Declaration of Human Rights (1948), which has been endorsed by many nations. Among those rights are freedom of thought and freedom of religion. Yet, despite the most formal affirmations of laws, those rights continue to be violated in practice by countless administrative or bureaucratic restrictions. Those restrictions entail the oppression of whole populations, cultural alienation, and even the debasing of an elementary sense of ethics in many cases.

The right to culture is linked historically to the rights of *the nation* as such and to the "fundamental sovereignty of society that manifests itself in the culture of the nation." For every individual, the nation is the milieu that generates its culture: "The nation exists through culture and for culture, hence it is the great educator of human beings so that they can be more in the community. It is this community that possesses a history that goes beyond the history of the individual and the family."[15]

The Church, which has been called *mater et magistra* ("mother and teacher"), essentially has an impact on culture through education; and it is by safeguarding the primary value of education that the Church defends the culture of the human being. Education is, first and foremost, the formation of the human spirit and its moral conscience, which are the highest manifestations of human culture: "There is no doubt that the primary and fundamental cultural reality is the spiritually mature human being: the fully educated human being, the human being capable of educating oneself and others. Nor is there any doubt that the primary and fundamental dimension of culture is a healthy morality: *moral culture.*"[16]

Thus the Church appeals to the conscience of all men and women, seeking the triumph of reason and wisdom in human relations and the general reassertion of the principle that "the human being infinitely surpasses itself," for each person is unique and open to the transcendent. As John Paul II put it: "May our contemporaries again find the taste and esteem for culture, the true victory of reason, for fraternal understanding and sacred respect for the human being capable of love, creativity, contemplation, solidarity, and transcendence."[17]

TOWARD A FULL DEFINITION OF THE HUMAN BEING

The deeper motivation of Christians involved in the defense of the human being is embedded in the gospel message itself, because there is an organic and essential link between Christianity and Culture: "The whole set of assertions about the human being is part of the very substance of Christ's message and the mission of the Church."[18] The Church addresses itself not just to humanity in general but also to human beings in their concrete, unique, historical, unrepeatable reality. This specific human being and every human being are created in the likeness of God, loved and chosen by God from all eternity, and saved by Jesus Christ.

Paul VI used strong terms to explain why the Church comes to the defense of the integral human being. Speaking to artists in 1964, he said that the Church regards itself as the guarantor of humanity and feels deeply wounded by anything and everything that undermines human integrity. All that offends us, he said, "we who are the guardians of humanity in its entirety, of the plenary definition of the human being, of the human being's healthy morality and stability."[19] That says it all; and the reason is that the Church defends the human being in its fullest and most complete sense. The Church stands for a "complete definition of the human being."

The merit of Vatican II was that it put the human being and its future at the center of its concerns. At the closing of that council, Paul VI underlined that fact. At the heart of the council's deliberations, he said, lay the Church's interest in the human being itself: "The Church of this council has been deeply preoccupied with the human being . . . as it really is presented in our age: the living human being, the human being wholly preoccupied with self, the human being who not only makes itself the center of all its interests but dares to present itself as the principle and ultimate reason of all reality. The whole phenomenal human being—garbed in its countless guises—has stepped out before the assembled council fathers, as it were."[20]

Paul VI rejected the criticisms that this identification with the human being could have evoked from some, to the effect that the Church had deviated toward "the anthropological positions assumed by modern culture." The Church's humanism, on the contrary, is a humanism open to the transcendent: "Our human-ism becomes Christianity, and our Christianity turns theocentric, even though we can likewise say that to know God we must know the human being."[21]

This theme is continuously echoed by John Paul II. Our uncon-ditional love for the human being is rooted in our adhesion to Christ. This radical adherence commits us to serve the human being in cooperation with every person of good will: "Sincere adhesion to Christ has as its normal consequence unconditional passion for the human being, its defense and its authentic betterment. And it is on the basis of this commitment to the human being that we can undertake encounter, dialogue, and collaboration with those who do not share the same religious faith but who do hold as their own the fundamental values associated with the dignity of the human being."[22]

Since Vatican II in particular, the Church has managed both to welcome and to enrich the social, anthropological, and historical reflection of our day. It has managed to see the rise of culture to prominence as a deep-rooted human aspiration and to ally itself with the human being in its legitimate struggles and hopes. One cannot help but think of Cardinal Newman's prediction in the nineteenth century. He foresaw that one day the Church would become the last refuge of human culture. Paul VI pointed this out to Jean Guitton: "You recall the splendid comment of Newman: the time will come when the Church alone will defend the human being in human culture."[23]

Without claiming any exclusiveness for the Church in the de-fense of *the human*, we can see that it now appears before the world as the natural ally of all those men and women who are dedicating themselves to human betterment.

4/The Links between Culture, Justice, and Peace

When we talk about "defending culture," some persons immediately raise this question: Is not the promotion of culture an insidious way of retrieving the fight for justice? This ambiguous question must be given a clear-cut answer. We must show that the struggle for justice and the fight for culture are the two sides of one and the same goal. The facts speak for themselves. By way of example, consider the vicissitudes of all the efforts on behalf of development over the past thirty years or so.

CULTURAL FACTORS IN DEVELOPMENT

After countless initiatives against poverty and human misery, humanitarian organizations, governments, and societal officials have come to realize that their efforts are in vain so long as they neglect the *cultural factors* affecting the complicated process embodied in the development of a people. The cultural element plays a crucial role among both the givers and receivers of international aid. The facts themselves tell us it is a mistake to reduce the problems of justice or development to economic processes, a mere balance of forces, or a reversal of the existing balance between the dominant and the dominated. The first development programs drawn up by the international community were too exclusively focused on the economic and technical aspects of development; they slighted or ignored the cultural factors involved. Although huge sums of money were invested in the fight against poverty, the poor peoples of the world drew meager benefits from the projects. We discovered that the countries of the Third World attached more importance to their identity and cultural liberation than to the introduction of models of industrialization and urbanization proposed to them by the affluent nations. The poor peoples have their own dignity and culture, we learned, and they will often refuse economic and technical aid, even food, if such aid jeopardizes their traditional culture.

These facts, which can be seen in more than one Third World country, raise a basic issue: the meaning of development. The Church reminds us that progress cannot be conceived as merely economic, quantitative growth focusing on efficiency and self-interest. *Qualitative* and *cultural* goals are just as important for the growth of societies. As Paul VI put it in *Octogesima Adveniens*:

> Attention has certainly been called, and with good reason, to the limits and bad effects of economic growth that is framed solely in terms of the quantity of wealth; persons are also looking for benefits of a qualitative nature. The form and authenticity of human interrelationships and the degree of responsible participation are as significant and important for the future of society as the quantity and variety of goods produced and consumed.[1]

The Christian view of social progress stresses that the pursuit of justice cannot be separated from the cultural promotion of humankind. Those who set up an opposition between *culture* and *justice* claim that extolling culture is merely an evasion or excuse for neglecting the practical fight for justice. Now we cannot deny that an intellectualist temptation does exist at times, taking the form of a false spiritualism or angelism. It has often been denounced by the Church and by the bishops of Latin America, at their Puebla Conference especially. But we must be careful to avoid falling into the opposite mistake as well: the temptation to view the fight for justice in a materialistic perspective.

Justice and *culture* must grow together. When he created the Pontifical Council for Culture, John Paul II stressed "the cultural conditions that underlie the development of peoples. It is becoming increasingly clear that cultural progress is intimately bound up with the construction of a more just and fraternal world."[2] The whole social teaching of the Church must be interpreted in this perspective. In it social, economic, political, and technical problems are viewed from a standpoint that gives privileged consideration to the meaning of the human being and its culture. Since Vatican II and the teachings of Paul VI and John Paul II in particular, the cultural aspect of development has become an integral part of the Christian view of progress for both individuals and societies. Moreover, the promotion of justice must be viewed in the context of a new civilization that must be built. Paul VI stated this explicitly: "The social questions introduced by the present-day economic course include such matters as these: human conditions in production, equitable interchange of goods and distribution of wealth, the significance and impact of increased consumption needs, and the sharing of work responsibility. Such problems must be framed in the broader context of a new civilization."[3]

TWO ENCYCLICALS ON CULTURE AND PROGRESS

The most important Church documents on the development of peoples are Paul VI's encyclical *Populorum Progressio* (1967) and *Sollicitudo Rei Socialis* published by John Paul II twenty years later.[4] Both documents can be properly understood only if they are read in a clearly cultural perspective. It is consistently against *the horizon of culture and civilizations* that these encyclicals deal with such matters as justice, co-responsibility, and fellowship.

In the opening of his letter, Paul VI expresses the Church interest and concern for the cultural development of peoples: "This is particularly true in the case of those peoples who are trying to escape the ravages of hunger, poverty, endemic disease, and ignorance; of those who are seeking a larger share in the benefits of civilization and a more active improvement of their human qualities; of those who are consciously striving for fuller growth." Paul VI's key expression here is "the complete development of the human being and the joint development of all humanity."[5] He has in mind complete human development and progress on both the individual and the collective levels. The two aspects are inseparable: "Complete development of the human individual necessarily entails a joint effort for the development of the human race as a whole."[6] Before concluding his encyclical, Paul VI stresses the point again because it involves the future of civilization: "We must travel this road together, united in minds and hearts. We feel it necessary to remind everyone of the seriousness of this issue. . . . At stake are the survival of countless innocent children, more human living conditions for countless destitute families, world peace, and the future of civilization."[7] The key theme of *Populorum Progressio* is also expressed in another formula, the development of *every human being and of the whole human being*: "The development we speak of cannot be restricted to economic growth alone. To be authentic, it must be well-rounded; it must foster the development of every human being and of the whole human being."[8]

My aim in this chapter is not to offer a systematic presentation of the Church's teaching on justice, development, or peace. It is to point up how much stress that teaching puts on the *cultural dimension of progress*. Close examination of *Populorum Progressio* and *Sollicitudo Rei Socialis* convinces us of this. On almost every page of their letters, Paul VI and John Paul II allude to "culture", "civilization", and "humanism" to make clear that no development worthy of the name is possible without an understanding of the cultural conditions involved in the progress of peoples. Here we have the key to reading and interpreting these messages on development. Has that point been brought out enough in our commentaries on these encyclicals? Are we not still overlooking the Popes' appeal, which managed to bring together the demands of justice and those of culture in such a dynamic way?

Paul VI views development in the most realistic perspective possible. He repeatedly calls attention to the *moral realities* underlying any and all human progress. Culture, development, and peace are one, and Paul VI expressed that fact in a phrase that caught the popular imagination: "development is the new name for peace."

It should be clear to readers, then, that this encyclical devoted wholly to development, justice, and peace remains scrupulously attentive to the *cultural preconditions for progress*.

DEVELOPMENT AND THE CULTURE OF SOLIDARITY

Neither justice nor development can be won solely by economic planning or technological projects. Nor does justice result automatically from violent action. To establish a situation of justice in the world, said Paul VI, we simply must build "a civilization of worldwide solidarity." In other words, human beings must come to the aid of their brother and sister human beings. We must promote the worlwide conscience of the human family.

We must simultaneously have an impact on the *culture* of both the oppressed and the oppressors, both the rich and the poor, both the givers and receivers of aid, both the affluent nations and those who yearn to escape their poverty. "The hungry peoples of the world cry out to the peoples blessed with abundance. And the Church, cut to the quick by this cry, asks each and every human being to hear their brother's and sister's plea and answer it lovingly."[9] In these words we discover the deepest import of the Church's teaching on justice and development. In the last analysis, it is a plea for human fraternity. There will be no authentic development unless we reunite the *cultural dynamism* of the affluent peoples and that of the poor peoples. Among more affluent peoples there must be a thoroughgoing cultural reexamination, so that they may criticize the values of their consumer society and pay heed to their fellow human beings who are needy and impoverished. Cultural changes are also necessary in the countries yearning for access to modernity. They will have to welcome the values of industrial and technological society without sacrificing the essentials of their ancestral traditions.

We can see, then, that the struggle for justice cannot be dissociated from the promotion of a more humane society. It comes down to serving every human being and all human beings. To forget this elementary principle would be to end up with solutions negating the spiritual and the human. For the Church, justice and humanism go hand in hand:

> The ultimate goal is a full-bodied humanism. And does this not mean the fulfillment of the whole human being and of every human being? A narrow humanism, closed in on itself and not open to the values of the spirit and to God who is their source, could achieve apparent success, for human beings can set about organizing terrestrial realities without God. But "closed off from God, they will end up being directed against the human being. A humanism closed off from other realities becomes inhuman." True humanism, then, must be open to the Absolute.[10]

So it would be false to set in opposition the exigencies of justice and those of culture, because the work of justice is one of the highest achievements of humanism. Indeed, it is a work of civilization and human elevation. It is clear from the above observations that the elementary needs of the human being are not simply physical or material; they are equally spiritual and cultural in nature. To be sure, human beings have a basic need for food, tender care, and safe shelter; but they have an equally basic need to know, to understand their changing world, and to have their identity respected so that they can grow and assert themselves in their culture. And so human beings yearn, with all their might, to satisfy their elementary needs for justice and culture at the same time.

Twenty years after *Populorum Progressio*, John Paul II has strongly reasserted the validity of a conception of development respecting the cultural and spiritual dimension of the human

being. An overview of John Paul's cultural approach to development can thus be summarized from his encyclical *Sollicitudo Rei
Socialis* (1987).

The tasks of development have grown even more dramatic and
urgent in the last twenty years. Poverty today has in fact worsened
and become more widespread in many parts of the world, and the
increased speed of social change has made the inequality between
human beings even more appalling. Millions of human beings
today live without hope. John Paul II has used the expression
"living without hope" on a number of occasions in order to
describe the human tragedy of extreme poverty. We must therefore make a fresh moral evaluation of the *type of poverty* that
oppresses so many of our brothers and sisters, and its implica-
tions. There is material indigence or the lack of essential goods so
that life is reduced to a subhuman level. However, there is also the
poverty caused by violent denial of the elementary rights of *social,
cultural* and *religious freedom*—a poverty that can be extremely
serious and can indeed cause even more suffering than material
poverty. It is therefore clear that the task of development involves
not only the countries of the third world, but all countries in which
men and women are physically, culturally and spiritually oppressed.
The sovereignty and cultural identity of every people constitute
fundamental objectives of human advancement. Although the
preferential option and love for the poor are concerned particularly
with the Third World, we must not ignore the great number of
people who are oppressed by economic and cultural privation and
treated without proper respect even in the wealthier countries.
Development concerns *all the poor* in the world.

The various forms of poverty are exacerbated today by the fact
that everybody feels oppressed by the unbearable tensions between the *ideological blocs* of East and West which constitute a
gigantic impersonal mechanism dividing the world with the dis-
astrous consequence that vast resources are committed to military
or "defense" programs, which in turn deprives the human family
of the means necessary for the development of all.

The very realistic analysis of the present forms of underdevelopment leads us to recognize that the various types of poverty of our
times have their roots in political factors, and in the final analysis
in a moral ill brought about by the sins and omissions of many
people. We are all called to a deep collective conversion; each man
and woman is called to a generous examination of his or her own
moral behavior in the perspective of the phenomenon of poverty

and underdevelopment. The challenge of development can thus be seen in all its gravity as a call to *universal solidarity*, which is the only dynamic reality capable of redefining true progress on the basis of the individual's authentic being. If we take economic objectives or the accumulation of material goods as our sole aim, we are betraying the true tasks of development.

Christians are convinced that faced with the challenge of development the light of the Gospel will eventually succeed in transforming the dominant cultures that act as a scandalous brake on efforts at joint advancement and threaten the future in the world. We must overthrow the *culture of consumerism*, oppressive ideologies and simple resignation in the face of the suffering and poverty of the masses; in its place we are called to establish a *culture of solidarity* and effective commitment to serving the good of the whole human family. Those who help bring about peace and justice will not be lacking in hope. Never before have the poor had such need of hope. The Gospel will imbue consciences with this *culture of hope* for liberation from every type of material, political and spiritual oppression.

John Paul's encyclical confirms therefore and expands with new arguments the cultural, ethical and spiritual dimensions of development, which Paul VI had underlined twenty years before.

These anthropological perspectives also have ethical import. They pose a radical challenge to civilizations that allow themselves to be carried away by the primacy of materialism, consumerism, or hedonism. John Paul II had often stressed this point, which is so fundamental for the reflection of our contemporaries. Two types of civilizations confront each other. One gives a privileged place to *having*, to materialistic satisfactions. The other upholds the loftiest values of a human being concerned about its fellow human beings, the neediest in particular. Human dominion over the universe of things is not enough. The human being cannot renounce its own proper role in the human family. If it forgets its fellow human beings in the quest for material goods, it will destroy its own humanity. It will become the slave of illusory riches and sink into vile egotism. That is the temptation facing affluent societies:

> A purely materialistic civilization condemns the human being to a slavery of that sort, even if that runs counter to the intentions and principles of its makers. This problem is certainly at the root of the concern that our contemporaries feel for the human being. It is not simply a matter of giving an abstract answer to the question: What is

the human being? It has to do with the whole dynamism of life and civilization.[11]

John Paul II contrasts the civilization of consumption with the plight of multitudes who are suffering and dying in poverty.

The *culture of affluence* is radically challenged by the *culture of poverty* because all human beings today are ultimately faced with the essential question: What exactly is true progress for human beings? In the framework of this progress, asks John Paul II, "are human beings as such becoming truly better: more spiritually mature, more aware of the dignity of their humanity, more responsible, more open to others, especially the weakest and the neediest, more ready to give, more inclined to offer their aid to all?"[12]

CULTURE AND JUSTICE: INSEPARABLE

The Church's reflection on the exigencies of justice in the world rightly stresses the interrelationship between culture, education, the promotion of development, the fight against hunger, and action for justice and peace. As John Paul II told UNESCO, we are dealing with "a vast system of communicating vessels."[13] In the name of justice itself, the Church rejects all humanisms that are closed in on themselves, because they ultimately end up betraying the human being.

Underlying the thought and social action of Christians is an anthropological vision. John Paul II reiterated it at the Puebla Conference: "Let us also keep in mind that the Church's activity in such areas as human promotion, development, justice, and human rights is always intended to be in the service of the human being, the human being as seen by the Church in the Christian framework of the anthropology it adopts."[14] He urged the bishops at the Puebla Conference to explore the links between evangelization and human promotion or liberation.[15] The guiding principle ever remains that of considering the human being in terms of its whole being and its concrete, historical situation, and in such a way as to respect *"the truth about Christ, the Church, and the human being."*[16]

From the Church's viewpoint, then, liberation could not possibly be confined to a single dimension of the human being, however important we may consider that dimension to be: the economic, political, social, or cultural dimension. The whole human being must be completely liberated on both the material and the spiritual level. To forget that fact is to pave the way for new idols and new oppressions that will afflict the peoples of the world.[17]

To be sure, the Church does not impose its anthropology on all human beings. The vision of the human being inspiring it derives from its faith in a God who has created human beings in God's own image and likeness. But the Church addresses itself to all persons of good will who picture the human being as a sacred being worthy of unconditional respect. It begs them to recognize what Paul VI called "the radical limits of economics"; despite the immense services that economics can render to the human being, it is in danger of "absorbing human capabilities and freedom to an excessive degree." We must move on from the economic dimension to the political and cultural dimensions.

To frame the task of development in the perspective of universal solidarity is to somehow move beyond a too narrowly "national" view of the fight for justice and to underline its "global" perspective. Some are inclined to put almost exclusive stress on domestic action within each nation: efforts to arouse a sense of responsibility in national government, intermediate bodies, social groups, representatives of capital, and workers. Such aims and efforts are always valid, but insufficient. The question of justice has now taken on a global dimension. Paul VI vigorously underlined this point in *Populorum Progressio*, and John Paul II has reiterated it in clear, unmistakeable terms. In *Populorum Progressio* Paul VI said bluntly: "Today it is most important to understand and appreciate that the social question ties all humans together, in every part of the world."[18]

Without denying the dynamism of nations, groupings, and social classes, we must realize that the problems of justice and development involve the human family as a whole. This is a fundamental socio-cultural change. In *Laborem Exercens*[19] John Paul II writes: "If in an earlier day one focused on the problem of 'class' in connection with this question, in more recent times it is the problem of the 'world' that takes center stage." Development presupposes moral action involving ties of solidarity between all human groups. It is a matter of conscience and a new culture. Justice calls for fellowship, and vice versa.

We do well to highlight the humanist and cultural dimension of this view of justice and progress. John Paul II's encyclical *Laborem Exercens* deserves a careful rereading in terms of that interpretive grid. In it we find, in particular, a clear statement that human work is the basis of all social and cultural development: "Human work is a key, probably the essential key, to the whole social question, if we try to see it from the standpoint of human welfare." If the basic problem is "to make life more humane, then the key that is human work takes on basic and crucial importance." Work is, in fact, bound up with the loftiest values underpinning society: the family, education, the progress of society at large. "The family is both a community made possible by work and the first internal school of work for every human being." Work creates the cultural patrimony of societies, nations, and the human family. "The result . . . is that the human being links its deepest human identity with member-ship in its nation. It also sees in its work a means of adding to the common good elaborated by its fellow countrymen, realizing that work thereby helps to multiply the patrimony of the whole human family and of all human beings living in the world." The primary dignity of human work lies in "the fundamental truth that the human being, created in God's image, participates in the Creator's work through its own work." Christians are convinced that their labor has liberative and redemptive value because, by dedicating themselves to creative work, they participate in the paschal mys-tery and commit themselves to the kingdom of God. "Their work has an impact, not only on *terrestrial progress*, but also on the development of *the kingdom of God* to which we all are called by the power of the Holy Spirit and the word of the gospel message."

Some persist in believing that such a conception of justice and development will paralyze all action and concrete commitment. They see it as nothing but a utopia or a dream condemning the generous-hearted to ineffectiveness. What matters, they say, is the rough and tumble struggle for justice. But we are convinced otherwise, by what has been seen above. Utopia, we feel, lies closer to justice without humanism. What is at stake here is the very effectiveness of the struggle for justice.

To accept a straitened vision of justice would be to overlook the mobilizing power of an *ethical ideal* capable of triggering the con-crete forms of collaboration that justice and development require. John Paul II made the point in Hiroshima: "The construction of a more just humanity or a more united international community is not a mere dream or an impractical ideal. It is a moral imperative, a sacred duty. And the intellectual and spiritual genius of humanity must face up to it by undertaking a general mobilization of talents and strengths, and implementing all the technical and cultural resources of the human race."[20]

These teachings of Paul VI and John Paul II on justice, develop-

ment, peace, and human rights, expounded with feelings of anxiety and urgency, both reflect and deepen the declarations of
Vatican II. In three particularly rich sections of *Gaudium et Spes* we
find the same lines of thought. The goal "must be service to the
human being, indeed to the whole human being, viewed in terms
of material needs and the demands of intellectual, moral, spiritual,
and religious life; and when we say the human being, we mean
every human being whatsoever and every group of human beings,
of whatever race and from whatever part of the world." Development must be kept under the control of humanity and not left "to
the sole judgment of a few individuals or groups having excessive
economic power, or of the political community alone, or of certain
especially powerful nations." By very realistic fashion the Church
recognizes the role that might be played by economics: "Technical
progress must be fostered, along with a spirit of initiative, an
eagerness to create and expand enterprises, the adaptation of
methods of production, and the strenuous efforts of all who
engage in production." But a higher principle remains: serving the
whole human being by respecting *personal rights* and the *culture* of
each and every people.[21]

In our present historical situation, then, action on behalf of
justice, development, and peace shows up as an undertaking that
presupposes what Paul VI and John Paul II called "a new culture of
solidarity." It is cultures themselves that must be changed if justice
is to become operative, if injustices are to be combated effectively.
At bottom this *cultural conception of development* is the only realistic
one because it alone appeals to the deepest dynamics of our
societies and to the psychology of our contemporaries. The demand made to this generation is that it be wise enough to put all its
resources and technical know-how in the service of the whole
human being and every human being. From the Christian standpoint there can be no antimony between the promotion of justice
and the promotion of culture. Instead we must realize that this
twofold, inseparable quest is the one and only way to serve the
concrete human being without betraying its dignity and its highest
aspirations.

TOWARD A CULTURE OF PEACE

What about the problem of peace? It is indeed difficult to deal
with it objectively and in an ethical perspective. Here Christians
can make an indispensable contribution. Let us take note of the

fact that when the Church considers questions of peace and disarmament, it always adopts an approach that is clearly *ethical* and *cultural*.

The document that best illustrates the thinking of the contemporary Church on peace is John XXIII's encyclical *Pacem in Terris* (1963). I noted its importance and impact in chapter 2. That encyclical was not addressed solely to Catholics but to all persons of good will; and the pope's words linked up with one of the deepest yearnings of present-day culture. When he writes about the rights of individuals and peoples, we find him repeatedly alluding to "cultural rights" and "cultural benefits." At the end of each major section or part, John XXIII brings out the expectations of present-day culture by describing "signs of the times" that reveal the hopes of our contemporaries: the economic and cultural promotion of workers, the social responsibility of women, the independence of nations, the formulation of human basic rights, recourse to negotiation to still the terror of arms, and the awareness of belonging to a global community. Peace is essentially a work of justice, love, and human culture. One cannot understand the import of this major encyclical if one overlooks its cultural and ethical aims. And this approach prevails in all the more recent Church declarations on peace.

Let us remember Paul VI's succinct formula in *Populorum Progressio* (1967): "development is the new name for peace." It sums up his whole thinking on economic and cultural development as the foundation for peace. When it comes to defining peace or its preconditions, he invoked the cultural aspect. On December 8, 1974, Paul VI said that peace is an integral part of humanism: "True humanism and true civilization lie in the interiorization of peace." War is anticivilization, as it were, the opposite of civilized society. And Paul VI went on to say: "In a word, weapons and wars must be excluded from the undertakings of civilizations."[22]

Addressing UNESCO, John Paul II noted that the nuclear menace could lead to "the destruction of the fruits of culture and the products of civilization that have been produced over the centuries by successive generations of human beings who believed in the primacy of the spirit and never relented in their efforts or their labors."[23] Speaking in Hiroshima, he noted that war would likely "destroy the human family . . . and all the achievements of civilization."[24] Peace is patiently constructed by the spiritual genius of humanity: "Peace is one of the loftiest achievements of culture, and for that reason it deserves all our intellectual and

spiritual energy."[25] To be faithful to its mission, the Church dedicates itself totally to the defense of peace, which is one of the most precious benefits of human culture.

On June 11, 1982, John Paul II addressed a message to the second special session of the UN general assembly on disarmament. In it he explored these same ideas further: "In our day perhaps no question touches so many aspects of the human condition as the question of arms and disarmament." He mentioned the scientific, technical, social, and economic aspects as well as political problems and relationships between governments. He went on to say: "Moreover, our worlwide system of armaments greatly affects cultural developments. Crowning everything are the spiritual questions that have to do with the very identity of the human being and its choices for the future and later generations."[26] He implored governments not to rest content with rhetoric, with the idiom of threats and counterthreats, as a kind of psychological war between peoples. That game could prove fatal: "The history of civilizations offers us terrifying examples of what happens when that course is tried."[27]

The Church adopts a realistic attitude. It knows that we cannot talk about disarmament without reaching agreements on arms reduction. But it never stops repeating that the most important work, perhaps the slowest but also the most important, must be done in the area of spiritual values and the collective conscience of peoples. To reverse the present arms race, notes John Paul II, there must be a parallel effort on two fronts: "On the one hand, an immediate and urgent effort by governments to progressively reduce armaments in an equitable way. . . . On the other, a more patient but no less necessary effort focusing on the conscience of peoples, getting them to realize the ethical cause of the insecurity that breeds violence: the material and spiritual inequalities of our world." For the Church, disarmament has to do not only with the engines of death but also with the human spirit and the culture of human beings. As John Paul II put it to the United Nations, there must be a "disarmament of the engines of death" and a "disarmament of human spirits."[28]

At this crucial point in human history the construction of peace shows up as the highest achievement of culture. Peace is essentially the work of the enlightened human conscience. There is no peace without human culture. And without peace, culture could not possibly survive.[29] Only by the humanization of our societies will we be able to establish a true *culture of peace*. No objective is

more urgent or more difficult. But let us not forget that culture is equally a form of hope. Believers must bear living witness to the world that peace is first built in human spirits and by spiritual means. This conviction was strikingly affirmed by world religious leaders when they met in Assisi for a day of prayer (October 27, 1986), at the invitation of John Paul II. He underlined the significance of the events: "More than ever before in history, it is evident to all that there is an intrinsic connection between a truly religious outlook and the great boon of peace."[30]

5/Governments and their Cultural Policies

Culture embodies the loftiest values of individual persons and living communities. It is their reason for being and their hope. But culture is not merely an ideal. In concrete reality it often becomes the expression of contradictory interests, the object of political struggles and confrontations. One particular problem that now causes increasing uneasiness is government intervention in the cultural domain. Some are fearful of the state or government as culture advocate, educator, provider of information, or provider of social welfare in general. Others, however, are pleased with the commitment and involvement of governments in behalf of culture.

What criteria of judgment can we use vis-à-vis the cultural policies of modern governments? Here citizens confront a vast domain where their vigilance and action could be crucial in ensuring a truly democratic promotion of culture. This will be my topic in the present chapter. Let me begin with some facts.

THE GROWTH OF CULTURAL POLICIES

Today we are seeing a notable development in political practice: present-day governments are showing an increasingly marked interest in the realm of culture. More than a hundred countries now have a ministry of culture or an official organism devoted to cultural affairs. Of course, governments have always paid some attention to culture, if only to safeguard their national heritage, their historical sites and monuments, their literary and artistic traditions. The new feature we see today is the fact that government intervention in the domain of culture has become considerably broader and more specialized. This development is more understandable if one recalls the expansion of the whole notion of culture, as discussed in chapter 1 of this volume.

In an earlier day governments interpreted "culture" to mean the various embodiments of artistic, literary, and intellectual creation. Now they have broadened the notion of culture by giving it an anthropological sense. It is viewed as *the identity of a collectivity* and its typical ways of thinking, acting, believing, and living. For governments, then, culture now includes the two aspects, classic and sociological, that I examined earlier.

The problems inherent in cultural policies are prompting ongoing studies and some interesting meetings at the international level. Worthy of special note are the UNESCO world conferences on cultural policies, held in Venice in 1970 and in Mexico in 1982. Let me also mention the many regional or international conferences of various government ministries of culture: for example, the one held by the countries making up the Council of Europe in 1984; it took place in West Berlin and issued a *European Declaration of Cultural Objectives*. Similar meetings have taken place in Scandinavia, Latin America, Asia, the Near East, and Africa. At the African meeting, *A Cultural Charter for Africa* was approved in 1976. Muslim countries are similarly investing their concerted efforts in the Islamic Organization for Education, Science, and Culture (ISESCO). It is in Europe that ministries of culture are more active. Their ministers meet regularly every two or three years.

A synthetic overview of current problems relating to cultural policies was put together by UNESCO at the international Mondiacult Conference held in Mexico in 1982.[1] Keeping all this in mind, we can see how the Church's thinking is responding to the demands for a cultural policy that respects human beings and aids societal progress.

THREE TYPES OF CULTURAL POLICIES

We can differentiate three types of cultural policies in the current practice of governments. For some governments cultural policy still is linked to the classic, esthetic conception of culture; it has to do with promoting education and the arts, and with taking care of national monuments, historical sites, libraries, and museums. In such cases the cultural realm mainly has to do with the nation's heritage and achievements of an artistic or intellectual nature.

A second type of cultural policy is much more comprehensive, and tends to be the prevalent one right now. Its aim is to establish *cultural democracy* by fostering the participation of as many persons as possible in both the production of culture and its benefits. Thus, culture is no longer a matter for the ministry of culture alone; it now includes such areas as education, communication, youth, the family, health, welfare, work, leisure, professional training, and continuing education. So cultural policy tends to pervade large sectors of the government where a "cultural" or humanitarian dimension is evident.

A third type or model of cultural policy is now beginning to take shape as the result of maturing ethical reflection. The new idea being stressed now is that government policy as a whole should display and pursue a *cultural priority*. In other words, cultural objectives should henceforth guide the direction of societal life as a whole, putting the human being once again at the center of policy concerns and political life. We now hear talk about the *cultural objectives of development*. Cultural policy is to move beyond mere *economism*, the myopic focus on economic factors alone that has all too often shackled the evaluations of private or public administrators.

While fully acknowledging the importance of economic factors in societal life, the Church can only endorse efforts to redefine economic interests in terms of the human being. In his encyclical *Laborem Exercens* John Paul II had this to say about work: "We must stress and spotlight the primacy of the human being in the production process, *the primacy of the human being over things*."[2] This is a fundamental principle for all politics and policy. Economics is in the service of the humankind and its culture. All levels of government should make this their norm: "This view should have a central place in *every sphere of social and economic policy* and at every level: national, intercontinental, and international."[3]

Therefore, we must encourage any and every cultural policy that again puts human beings and their aspirations—physical and spiritual, individual and societal—at the center of government social plans. As John Paul II said on the occasion of the Mexican conference on cultural policies: "All this helps us to realize that any authentic cultural policy must embrace humankind in its totality— that is, in all its personal and social dimensions, not overlooking the ethical and religious aspects. It follows, then, that cultural policies cannot abstract from the spiritual vision of the human being in the promotion of culture."[4]

A COMMON CONCEPTION OF CULTURE

What ultimately characterizes a cultural policy is its conception of the human being and its cultural development. Underlying any cultural policy is a certain definition of culture and a certain image of the human being. Let us look at the description of culture in the 1982 *Mexico Declaration*, which was approved by the 130 participating governments:

> "In its widest sense, culture may now be said to be the whole complex of distinctive spiritual, material, intellectual and emotional features that characterize a society or social group. It includes not only the arts and letters, but also modes of life, the fundamental rights of the human being, value systems, traditions and beliefs."[5]

Notice that this formulation is very close to the definition of culture in *Gaudium et Spes* (n. 53), which was considered in the last three sections of Chapter 1.

Looking at the definition of culture approved in the *Mexico Declaration*, we can discern the declared objectives of cultural policy insofar as participating governments are concerned. Further on we shall see that there can be serious gaps between professed intentions and actual practice. Right here, however, I want to explore the ways in which the *objectives* of a cultural policy can effectively dovetail with the exigencies of a Christian line of thought. But instead of offering a technical description of the many areas where government policy may intervene in cultural matters, I shall focus on the major aims that call for an *ethical choice*, zeroing in on the following topics: the promotion of cultural identity; defense of the national culture; respect for minority groups; cultural liberation; the creativity of groups and associations; access to culture; participation and cultural democracy; cultural rights; education, the family, and culture; the influence of the media and cultural industries on culture; and dialogue between cultures.

THE PROMOTION OF CULTURAL AND NATIONAL IDENTITY

A primary aim or objective is the promotion of cultural identity. The cultural identity of a human group is its feeling of belonging, its attachment to a tradition and human heritage made up of a collective memory, beliefs, customs, and ways of thinking, working, living, and believing. The culture of a collectivity is based simultaneously on fidelity to the past and constant renewal; and there is not necessarily any contradiction between cultural change and the preservation of a group's heritage. Indeed, a truly alive culture is the typical form of growth for any human community seeking to retain its self-identity.

Culture and Nation

Cultural identity is bound up with the specific human condition of a collectivity, and it represents an inalienable right. This radical right is naturally incorporated in a national culture, whose exigencies have precedence over any interests or ideologies that contradict the historical destiny of the nation. John Paul II solemnly reminded UNESCO of the intimate ties between culture and nation:

> The nation is, in effect, the larger community of human beings who are united by various ties, but especially by culture. The nation exists *"through"* culture and *"for"* culture, hence it is the great educator of human beings enabling them to *"be more"* in community.[6]

Karol Wotyla, pope of the Church and son of Poland, reminds us that his nation has been able to survive in history *"solely on the basis of its culture."* He champions this fundamental sovereignty for every nation, a sovereignty embodied in "the nation's culture." He pays homage to the cultures of ancient peoples and to the cultures of the newer nations, for those peoples basically draw their reasons for living from their cultures.

We thus can see the abhorrent contradiction of any government policy which, in the name of an ideology, a system of interests, or racist principles, tries to suffocate the cultural identity of a national or ethnic collectivity in order to dominate and paralyze it. Yet this is the plight of countless peoples humiliated by present-day oppressive regimes. We can also be aware of all the violence of racist policies that go by the name of "apartheid" or "ethnic intolerance," and which amount to antinatural action against numerous collectivities whose rights and cultures are violated. In such cases we can say that an anticultural policy is being implemented against those groups, which in some cases constitute the numerical majority in their countries.

The Culture of Minorities

We must recognize the complicated cultural problems that must be faced by nonhomogeneous national communities. They must often put up with federated governments and linguistic or ethnic pluralism, a situation aggravated today by advanced transportation and by migrations. A correct cultural policy must take due account of the cultural identity of minorities, migrants, and marginal groups, but without falling into a tutelary policy that makes of these human communities instances of folklore or ethnology.

A delicate and deliberate balance must be sought and maintained, one that respects the inalienable identity of each of the parties in a national collectivity. Cultural factors, in other words, must be given priority over other considerations of a political or economic nature. Cultural policy should find its inspiration in the living nation, with all the complexity of its elements. There we have the expression of a right that is now being affirmed more consciously by all human societies.

The basic, guiding principle can be put as follows: we must guarantee respect for cultural communities within the framework of the political community. Vatican II described this yearning, which is particularly strong among minorities today: "In many consciences there is a growing concern to preserve the rights of minorities within a nation, without the latter overlooking their obligations to the larger political community. Moreover, respect for those who profess a different opinion or religion is also growing day by day."[7]

Cultural Liberation

In the case of countries aspiring to national liberation, the elaboration of an effective cultural policy seems to be a favorite tool in the struggle against economic and cultural dependence. Decolonization must strike at the roots of the cultural domination that prevents peoples from being themselves in line with their traditions, their own destiny, and their desire to be a community. Economic development is certainly a vital necessity, but modernization cannot be pursued at the expense of cultural identity. Cultural impoverishment cannot be the counterpart of economic enrichment, whatever form the latter may take. The Church sees itself in solidarity with those peoples who are investing all their energy "in the effort and struggle to move beyond everything that condemns them to a marginal life," said Paul VI in *Evangelii Nuntiandi*, they must be liberated from "situations of economic and cultural neocolonialism that are sometimes just as cruel as the old political colonialism."[8]

PARTICIPATION AND CULTURAL DEMOCRACY

An authentic cultural policy will seek to expand participation in the benefits of culture and thereby further the ideal of cultural democracy. Culture will become a link between all the citizens, who will share the loftiest values of the collectivity and a concern for the common welfare of the nation.

Government action will take concrete shape in spelling out a general policy and specific projects regarding culture. But note that a political project having to do with culture finds its primary inspiration in the needs and aspirations of a living society. Government parties and organisms cannot serve as a substitute:

> Political activity—need we point out that we are dealing here with concrete action, not a theoretical doctrine?—should be grounded on a formulated societal project that is consistent in itself with regard to the means it will use and the plans from which it will operate. These plans should proceed from a full-fledged awareness of the human vocation and of the different forms it assumes in society.[9]

The role of government is not to dispense an ideology inculcating uniformity. There is no way in which culture can be "handed out" officially. Instead, government must promote the access of as many citizens as possible to the benefits of the nation's living culture and also permit them to contribute to its enrichment. In this area especially, the power and authority of government is grounded on the free collaboration of the citizenry. The government acts "primarily as a moral force dependent on a people's liberty and sense of responsibility."[10] Of course, as societies grow more and more complex, government intervention will often be necessary to ensure the cultural development of all persons and all groups.[11]

The political community justifiably has a role in offering impetus and encouragement, but it must ever keep in mind that the ultimate goal is the elevation of the human being. The practical ways in which the political community structures itself and regulates public authority may vary in accordance with the particular character of a people and its historical development: "But these methods should always serve to form human beings who are civilized, peace-loving, and well disposed toward all—to the advantage of the whole human family."[12] In other words, government has an impact on the conditions fostering cultural democracy, but persons and groups are the agents and beneficiaries of cultural progress.

THE FUNDAMENTAL ROLE OF THE PERSON AND CULTURAL RIGHTS

The implementation of a cultural project on the societal level will be ethically acceptable insofar as it respects the needs of the human person and the family, and promotes a satisfactory educational policy. Defense of the inalienable cultural rights of the person is an urgent need in our day, and it is a presage of progress for human society as a whole. Signs of it will be progress in *liberty* and a *sense of responsibility*.

Recognition of this fact is what is prompting our contemporaries now to talk about *the cultural rights of citizens* and to include human rights in the notion of culture, as did the Mondiacult Conference. A detailed list of the principal rights can be found in John XXIII's encyclical, *Pacem in Terris* (1963). They would include, for example: the right to one's reputation; freedom of research and artistic creation; the right to information, education, work, decent housing, decent food, health care, and cultural opportunities; moral and religious freedom; the right to choose one's state in life, to set up a home, and to educate one's children; the right to associate, circulate freely, and express one's opinions.

All those rights belong to the individual, but they also have a social dimension. Hence it is difficult to make a clear-cut distinctions between individual rights and collective rights, which would include such rights as the following: the right to a homeland, justice, and peace; the right to free travel, regionally and nationally; the right to a healthy environment; and authorship rights, which pose difficult problems, especially with the spread of the media and the pirating of audiovisual productions. Governments must be mindful of the serious interests embodied in the cultural rights of both individual persons and social categories.

The political community will find it profitable to welcome all those groups trying to defend and promote cultural freedom and cultural rights. In particular, spiritual groups have a creativity of their own that can enrich societal life as a whole. To defend the rights of such groups is to contribute to the progress of culture in the highest and best sense of the term, which would include ultimate values: "It is up to cultural and religious groups—with due regard for the freedom of their members, of course—disinterestedly and in their own proper ways to nurture and foster in the social body their firm convictions concerning the nature, origin, and end of the human being and society."[13]

FAMILY, EDUCATION, CULTURE

Role of the Family

Another major imperative of any cultural policy is the defense and support of the family. This calls for a concerted effort at the highest levels of government by those in charge of cultural policy and those in charge of family policy. Besides being the cell that gives society its physical growth, the family is also the nucleus in which every living culture is rooted and grows. It is in the family that the child discovers its cultural identity, learns its native language—the main vehicle of culture—and becomes familiar with the elementary rules of sociability and fellowship. In every projected cultural policy, then, the family must be considered the privileged foundation for the transmission and enrichment of a people's wisdom, the soil in which are cultivated the ethical and spiritual values that give a living culture its fullest dignity. A new consciousness is emerging with regard to this matter. The family is now being seen as the subject of socio-cultural *rights* that cry out for an adequate governmental policy.[14]

At the West Berlin conference of European ministers of culture (May 1984), the Holy See's delegate stated the following: "In the advancement of culture a special role must be reserved for *the family*. This institution merits the fullest measure of government solicitude because the family always remains the natural cell and most suitable millieu for safeguarding such fundamental values as the native language, moral education, religious beliefs, a sense of social responsibility, and a sense of human fellowship."[15]

Education and Culture

Education is another crucial factor in cultural development, and most governments give it high priority in their policy-making. The challenge facing modern societies is keeping on top of things so that their educational policies respond in a timely way to new knowledge, new pedagogical advances, and the growing responsibilities of the citizenry, while still respecting the imperatives of their own cultures. As the Church sees it, progress in education and culture is the hallmark of any equitable socio-political system: "Thus, an indispensable condition for a just economic system is that it foster the growth and spread of public education and culture. The juster an economy is, the deeper will be its cultural awareness."[16]

An especially important and promising development is *continuing education*, which is considered by many to be one of the most notable cultural achievements of the past few decades. Cultural rights mean, first and foremost, the right of all citizens to an adequate education, whatever their age or condition may be.[17]

At the West Berlin conference mentioned above, the delegate for the Holy See said: "Let us note, in particular, the close, organic link between cultural development and *education*. . . . Among the cultural achievements of Europe, a special place must be reserved for *the school*, original creation of the European spirit and privileged means of cultural advancement and social progress. The school should remain linked to the free choice of families in the carrying out of their educational task."[18]

CULTURE AND THE MEDIA

An especially complicated problem facing governments is the relationship between the mass media and culture. The modern media have become an omnipresent power supported by what has come to be called the "culture industries." This term is broad enough to include all the producers of audiovisual materials and publications: movies, television, radio, books, periodicals, newspapers, video cassettes, records, computerized information, and data banks.

Any effective cultural policy must have a media policy because the media exert an ambivalent influence on culture. On the one hand the media represent one of the most remarkable achievements of modern culture: they are a remarkable expansion of communication possibilities among all human beings. They multiply in an unlimited way a people's chances to learn, to benefit from the treasures of art and science, and to share instantly in events that concern the whole human family. Thus, the modern media offer heretofore unimagined possibilities of promoting popular education and ongoing training, of stimulating interchanges and mutual understanding between groups, and of enriching the culture of a whole society. In many countries the media have become one of the most effective tools for ensuring literacy among the masses and furthering development.

On the other hand the modern media can also exert a negative influence on culture, and this fact rightly worries public authorities. One of their most frequently expressed concerns—and not just in Third World countries—is the fact that the steady importation of audiovisual programs ends up creating real cultural dependence. This leads to serious alienation from one's own native culture, and often to a serious decline in moral values, as well as a crumbling of traditional institutions, the family in particular.

The advent of the mass media confronts the political community with new obligations that are both inevitable and quite complicated. Faced with the media, modern governments cannot side-step the obligations imposed on them by public morality, the common good, and respect for a nation's culture.[19]

The media policies of governments differ in accordance with their ideological options, ranging from almost complete laissez-faire to authoritarian interventionism. Without entering into practical details, we can formulate *cultural norms for political choices*:

1. It is unacceptable that the only criterion for the development of culture industries should be their profitability or the law of the marketplace. Otherwise, cultural assets will sooner or later be shackled by the autonomous rule of economic calculation.

2. It is highly advisable for governments to pass appropriate measures that will encourage the production and distribution of cultural and educational programs, programs designed to foster cultural improvement and continuing education.

3. It also seems legitimate for a country to claim the right to impose on public broadcasters certain norms of professional ethics and moral decorum. Pure liberalism in this area soon turns into abuse and oppression.

4. It is desirable that countries exporting and importing cultural products examine their respective practices in terms of their international relationships and their respect for the cultural identity of every human group.

5. Particularly timely and relevant is the proposal to encourage bilateral or international cooperation in the production of audiovisual programs, each country getting across its own viewpoint and cultural choices.

6. Norms covering the importation of films and television programs seem now to be indispensable if countries are to reduce their dependence on foreign lands and foster cultural production at home.

7. In the long run, positive measures will undoubtedly prove to be the most effective ones. Such measures would include educating the public in good taste and a critical sense, and positively encouraging artistic creation as well as the production of works that express the spirit of each culture.

8. In the last analysis, any media policy must move beyond merely economic conditioning factors. It must spell out ethical criteria for the use of the media and promote the cultural quality of these new means of communication, which have now become part of the heritage of modern humanity.

At the West Berlin conference, the Holy See suggested the following norms:

> We do well to underline the *cultural aims* that can be promoted by the new communications media, notably by the use of satellites, cables, and video cassettes. Electronic devices for the mass media and information industry can no longer be developed exclusively in terms of profit. Governments are rightly concerned about *the new ethical and educational problems* posed by the systematic broadcasting of violence and moral degradation by some commercial media. We can only hope that satisfactory solutions will be found, solutions that respect the dignity and rights of citizens. The mass media have now become part of the cultural assets of modern collectivities, hence they should be made to serve *the uplifting of the whole human being and all human beings*.[20]

Perhaps in no other realm are ethics and culture so closely bound up with each other, as we all are coming to realize from actual experience.

EXTENT AND LIMITS OF CULTURAL POLICY

By way of conclusion, it might be well to spell out the nature of government intervention in cultural matters and its proper scope.

1. First, we must remember that cultural policy occupies an ever-increasing area in modern governments because *cultural aims* affect the whole range of activities undertaken by any government seeking to promote human values in and through all its policies.

2. Government action in the realm of culture must largely take the form of stimulus and encouragement rather than authoritarian measures. It is not for governments to determine the *content* or direction of culture. Culture is created by the vital groups of a nation, by families, schools, and institutions. The proper task of government is to *encourage* cultural creativity and the participation of as many citizens as possible in the benefits of culture: "It is not the function of public authority to determine what the proper nature or forms of human culture should be. It should rather foster the conditions and the means capable of promoting cultural life among all citizens and even within the minorities of a nation."[21]

3. We must recognize that cultural policy represents a real progress in the art of modern government, but we must also note that governments, especially in totalitarian states, often

use cultural activity as a tool for *ideological domination*. In such cases we have anticultural violence being perpetrated by the government and political parties: "It is not proper for governments or political parties solely concerned about themselves, to seek to impose their ideology by using means that would result in a dictatorship over human minds—truly the worst kind of dictatorship."[22]

One can only denounce the *perversion of politics* embodied in efforts by extremist regimes of the right or the left to use culture in order to effect the spiritual subjugation of whole populations. There we face one of the worst contradictions of our time: entire nations are being subjugated to ideological, political, or economic interests in the name of culture. This evil must be combatted openly and directly in the name of human fraternity: "Hence every effort must be made to ensure that culture is not diverted from its own purpose and made to serve political or economic interests."[23]

4. As we have seen, cultural policy is focused on one major objective: defending, encouraging, and promoting *cultural identity*. The goal is the cultural welfare of the nation, because it is in the nation that the specific heritage of each specific people is naturally fleshed out. By the same token, however, it must be pointed out that defense of one's cultural identity calls for an *openness to other cultures*. This is in the interest of one's national culture. Otherwise, a national culture is in danger of succumbing to narrowness and impoverishment insofar as it cuts itself off from other cultures, particularly in an age when civilization is becoming a global affair. Citizens should certainly love their homeland, but they must also be generous and open in their esteem for the whole human family: "Citizens should cultivate a generous and loyal devotion to their country, but without any narrowing of mind. At the same time, they should consider the welfare of the whole human family, which is tied together by the manifold bonds linking races, peoples, and nations."[24]

5. Governments will increasingly be spurred to coordinate their cultural policies. This is particularly true with respect to the media, because new communication technologies now overlap all geographical and cultural frontiers. Communication satellites, in particular, pose new problems of cultural policy to governments. Human activity in space, due to satellites or other instruments, raises many questions. And, as John Paul II has pointed out, these problems are not only technical and economic in nature but also "cultural, moral, and political."[25] One of the major services that can be performed by satellites

is the elimination of illiteracy and the promotion of popular culture. We must remember that approximately one billion human beings do not know how to read or write. In many instances, noted John Paul II, "culture can be spread only by means of images." Thus, satellites can contribute greatly to the spread of culture and promote the integral development of the human being.

But satellite transmission of culture cannot simply mean the imposition of the culture of affluent nations on developing countries. Some of the latter countries possess age-old cultures that must be preserved. They "must not become victims of an ideological colonialism that would destroy their traditions." Satellites should contribute, instead, to dialogue between cultures, such dialogue being of the utmost necessity for world peace.

John Paul II has also raised the ticklish issue of *cultural frontiers*: "Nations have cultural frontiers that are even more deeply entrenched than geographical or political frontiers. It should be possible to cross the latter frontiers because every human being is a citizen of the world and a member of the human family. But these frontiers should not be changed by violent means." By the same token, these frontiers should not prevent dialogue between one culture and another culture, nor "should they be violated by forms of cultural or ideological dictatorship." Space technology cannot be used to serve the aims of cultural imperialism or to undermine the authentic cultures of collectivities. These questions require dialogue among all the interested parties, especially among governments, which must show originality in their political approach to these new problems.[26]

6. Finally, we should note the relationships arising between government cultural policy and government foreign policy. A nation's culture is enriched by the contributions of all human cultures. Together, they form a common, indivisible heritage. Governments are becoming increasingly aware of this fact; that is why they are attaching growing importance to intercultural dialogue and exchange in their *foreign policy*. There is a growing conviction that *peace* is a joint cultural achievement, growing out of creative efforts by the human mind and spirit to respect all peoples in their diversity and their dignity. Peace is one of the most beautiful creations of culture.[27]

The highest motivation that can underlie government cultural policies is the notion that cultural promotion ultimately means service to the human being, a human being capable of moral responsibility, fellowship, and spiritual excellence. This was brought out by the governments that signed and issued the 1982 *Mexico Declaration*:

> It is culture that gives man the ability to reflect upon himself. It is culture that makes us specifically human, rational beings, endowed with a critical judgement and a sense of moral commitment. It is through culture that we discern values and make choices. It is through culture that man expresses himself, becomes aware of himself, recognizes his incompleteness, questions his own achievements, seeks untiringly for new meanings and creates works through which he transcends his limitations.[28]

These goals will require close cooperation between nations and governments. A World Decade for Cultural Development (1988–1997) has been decided by the United Nations and is now promoted by UNESCO. The Decade is setting itself *four major objectives*: 1) Drawing attention to the cultural dimensions of Development; 2) Affirmation and enrichment of cultural identities; 3) Increase in participation in cultural life; 4) Promotion of international cultural cooperation.

Four catchwords are to be retained: Cultural Dimension—Cultural Identity—Cultural Participation—Cultural Cooperation.

These objectives offer an important area for the cultural action of Christians, as we have seen in chapter 4 when we discussed the Church's conception of development. National and international cultural policies will need the inspirations of those who believe in the values of the Gospel for the development of societies.

Christians must appreciate the serious social and moral issues at stake in the modern practice of government cultural policies. All must be urged to become solidly *informed* about this new dimension of government policy and to be *sensitively aware of the ethical issues* involved. A vast field lies open to us if we are to carry out the cultural objective embodied in the Church's invitation, issued to all men and women of good will, to *defend humankind and its culture*. A new effort at education will be necessary.[29]

PART THREE

CULTURES AND THE GOSPEL MESSAGE

The encounter of the gospel message with human communities is culturally creative. Today there is a persistent concern to know what exactly is meant by "the evangelization of cultures." Chapter 6 explores this question, which the Church regards as vital for its activity in the present-day world. Pursuing this reflection further, I shall consider the problem of the "inculturation" of the gospel message. I shall examine it from a *socio-theological* standpoint in Chapter 7, and from the standpoint of the *Church's actual experience* with inculturation in Africa, Asia, and diverse cultural situations (Chapter 8). Concluding that survey, I shall formulate some basic propositions about inculturation deriving from the Church's reflection and concrete experience.

6/The Evangelization of Cultures

Cultural action by Christians takes place on two levels. One has to do with the defense of the human being as such, the other has to do with the evangelization of cultures. The latter expression raises difficulties in some environments because there is detected in it some sort of vague effort at collective indoctrination. Thus, it is important for us to know what exactly the Church means by "the evangelization of cultures." Let us recall what we saw in Chapter 1 and carefully differentiate the levels on which cultural action takes place.

At a first level, action on behalf of culture is action in the service of the human being as such, and for no other reason. It stems from a basic love for the human being, a love that can be shared by all persons of good will even those who do not profess any religion. Human fellowship, frankly and honestly recognized, is enough to inspire effective cultural action; indeed, such action is indispensable in our pluralistic societies. In the preceding chapters we have considered the many forms that cultural commitment can assume in defense of the human being and human culture.

On another level, cultural action is viewed in the specific perspective of the encounter between faith and cultures. This level certainly does not rule out the first level; but for Christian believers it represents a higher level of action that must be explored and understood better.

In this chapter and the two following ones I shall consider in what sense the Church's activity relating to cultures can be considered *evangelization*. Is this a mere linguistic analogy or is it an authentic evangelizing activity? Within this perspective we must consider what is meant today by the *inculturation* of the gospel message. Christian reflection and the Church's recent experience will help us to clarify these complicated questions, which lie at the heart of the Christian task of evangelization.

EVANGELIZATION AND THE SECULARIZATION
OF CULTURES

Let us note, first of all, that the relationships between faith and human cultures are now framed in a totally new perspective, due to the massive secularization that has taken place in the modern age. Before the advent of secularized societies, cultures were oriented around religious beliefs. These beliefs established the highest values of a given collectivity and provided the lives of individuals and societies with their ultimate meaning. Religion was the inspiration for their codes of conduct and gave direction to every area of life: the family, work, feasts and festivals, celebration of the major cycles of existence, the conception of law and public life, the accumulation and transmission of knowledge. The whole of individual and societal life had a religious meaning.

The secularization of modern cultures ushered in forms of cognition and rational thinking that are independent of religious representations of the universe, and it freed minds from archaic superstitions. But it often had the further effect of desacralizing human existence and cutting it off from the religious realm. Culture and religion no longer go together necessarily. This rupture has been felt as a dramatic event by the Church: "Undoubtedly, the rupture between gospel message and culture is the drama of our age, as it also was the drama of other ages."[1] This explains the growing realization among Christians that cultures as such must now become a field for evangelization.

But what might the "evangelization of cultures" mean? Properly speaking, is not evangelization directed solely at individual persons, who alone are capable of making the act of faith and converting to the gospel ideal? How can a culture adhere to the gospel message? In pluralistic societies how can cultures become objects of pastoral action? Such questions as these prompt us to spell out exactly how a culture can really become an object of evangelization.

First of all, it is well to point out that in the course of its history the Church has progressively expanded the horizons of its evangelizing work. From the very beginning the Church paid special attention to the poor, the sick, and the oppressed and later it created schools, universities, and hospitals. Progressively it felt that its field of pastoral action included education, rural life and the working class, specialized professions, social classes, public opinion, and the media. The Church always looked beyond a strictly individual-oriented version of its mission, therefore; it has also viewed as targets of evangelization groups, masses, and such collective realities as currents of thought and the mentalities of different social milieus. The Lord himself opened the widest possible horizons to the Church when he said: "Go and teach all nations." Hence the Church seeks to evangelize human beings in their concrete milieus and cultures. The Church, as Paul VI put it, seeks to convert simultaneously "the personal and collective conscience of human beings, the activities in which they engage, and the concrete milieus in which they live."[2]

The evangelization of cultures is not a new task for the Church. Throughout its history the Church has tried to carry the light of Christ into the heart of cultures and civilizations. But modern pluralistic society poses wholly new problems to the Church, as John Paul II has noted: "The concern to evangelize cultures is certainly not new for the Church. But it poses problems that are new in character in a world marked by pluralism, ideological clashes, and profound changes in human mentalities."[3]

WHAT DOES THE EVANGELIZATION OF CULTURES MEAN?

Having said that, let us now try to spell out the specific character of this task known as the evangelization of cultures.

PERCEIVING CULTURE AS A FIELD FOR EVANGELIZATION

Christians must first have a *mental perception of culture* as a human reality to be evangelized; they must be capable of listening to modern human beings "in order to understand them and invent a new kind of dialogue that will permit them to carry the originality of the gospel message into the very heart of present-day mentalities."[4] In other words, they must perceive mentalities, collective attitudes, as a specific field for evangelization.

Thus, evangelization must be understood in its full individual and societal sense. It is certainly true that only persons can make the act of faith, undergo conversion, receive baptism and the other sacraments, contemplate and worship God. But it is equally true, and we must recognize the fact, that evangelizing activity can go to the heart of cultures *through persons acting as intermediaries*: "We must evangelize—not in a superficial or merely decorative sense but in an in-depth way that goes to the roots—human culture and human cultures, understanding those terms in the broad, rich sense given them in *Gaudium et Spes*, always starting from the person and always returning to the relationship of persons with each other and with God."[5]

Christians today are beginning to realize that culture has become a proper field for evangelization. Vast cultural fields have never accepted or rejected the light of the gospel message. Respecting all human liberties but feeling the urgings of their faith, Christians now sense the urgency of proclaiming the Good News to today's world. As John Paul II put it: "We cannot not evangelize. Countless regions and cultural milieus remain unaware of the Good News of Jesus Christ. I am thinking of cultures in vast areas of the world that remain on the margins of the Christian faith. But I also have in mind vast cultural areas in traditionally Christian countries that today seem indifferent, if not resistant, to the gospel message."[6] The gospel message does its work essentially on the level of the values that characterize a culture and give it an ethical sense.

EVANGELIZING A CULTURAL ETHOS

We do well to grasp exactly which *cultural values* are capable of being enriched, purified, and perfected by the power of the gospel message. Every culture has tendencies and aspirations of its own that we must try to discover and explore in terms of their ethical and spiritual dimensions.

To put it more concretely, we must try to see how the gospel message can transform those dimensions of a culture having to do with *collective thinking and doing*: the typical behavior patterns of a milieu; the criteria of judgment; the dominant values and major interests; the habits and customs that leave their mark on worklife, leisure, and the practice of family, social, economic, and political life. As we can readily see, all these elements belonging to what is known as the *ethos* of a culture can be appreciated, evaluated, and given direction in the light of the gospel message. The ethos reveals the scale of values that gives more or less conscious direction to the behavior of a group. These codes of conduct, it should be noted, may not necessarily conform to the imperatives of objective morality. For example, a culture might regard as "normal" the superiority of one particular race, slavery, infanticide, or abortion. Thus the ethos leaves room for moral and spiritual progress on the level of individual conduct and on the level of group conduct. In secularized cultures a subtle dichotomy tends to take over here: the private sphere of individual conduct no longer seems to be connected with the public sphere. It is sometimes said that individual beliefs and convictions should not interfere with public forms of conduct and behavior. One can only denounce this "moral subjectivism," which actually comes down to amoralism and tends to become widespread in an ethos without transcendent values. Moreover, this view is clearly contradicted by experience. We can readily see that individual forms of behavior affect every social, ideological, or political movement. We need only ponder the impact of a creative initiative, a generous commitment, an act of disloyalty, or a moral scandal.

For their part, Christians are convinced that their faith can have a real impact on every sector of individual and collective life. While fully respecting the autonomy of terrestrial realities, they must also testify that the spirit of the gospel message really can transform individual behavior and the ethos of a society. To deny that would be to disavow the innovative power of the gospel message.

In large measure, then, evangelizing means detecting, criticizing, and even denouncing the aspects of a culture that contradict the gospel message and represent an attack on the dignity of the human being. With evangelical concern the Church gauges the distance that has opened up between modern cultures and itself. These cultures seem to be in danger of closing in on themselves, of succumbing to a kind of agnostic and immoral involution.[7]

John Paul II has often criticized the countervalues of present-day cultures and "the desires contrary to the Spirit that characterize so many aspects of contemporary civilization." He vigorously denounces "materialistic civilization," especially the dialectical and historical materialism that systematically rules out God's presence and activity in the human being and the world. Other "signs and signals of death" mark today's culture and call for a radical purification of human hearts and societies: abortion, euthanasia, warfare, terrorism. A new effort at evangelization is needed.

John Paul II reaffirms that the Spirit is at work in this world "subjected to the sufferings of time". Our civilization can hope for salvation. "Does there not rise up a new and more or less conscious plea to the life-giving Spirit from the dark shades of materialistic civilization, and especially from those increasing *signs of death* in the sociological and historical picture in which that civilization has been constructed?". In the end, "*there remains the Christian certainty* that the Spirit blows where he wills".[8]

Important as it is to denounce the antigospel and antihuman values that sometimes debase cultures, it is even more important to uncover the spiritual sensibility and expectations of present-day mentalities. We would do well, therefore, to understand what the gospel message means to modern psychologies. This is a crucial question for the Church, for it operates within cultures.

RESPONDING TO THE SECRET HOPES OF CULTURES

In a world like ours today, which is marked by widespread pluralism and agnosticism, the proclamation of the gospel message can paradoxically show up in all its *novelty*. Bearing witness to the salvation of all humans in Jesus Christ will link up with the secret hopes that lie buried but not dormant in the hearts of many of our contemporaries.[9]

The Church does not hesitate to state that the link between the gospel message and the human being helps to create culture "from its very foundation."[10] The Church, too, must help to "create culture in its relationship with the world." Thanks to the witness and commitment of Christians, faith becomes a culture that is lived. A symbiosis of cultural values and faith values takes place: "The synthesis of culture and faith is not just an exigency of culture but an exigency of faith as well. A faith that does not become culture is a faith that is not fully accepted, completely thought out, and truly lived."[11]

Evangelization, however, is not to be equated with the production of a culture or the creation of a civilization. Pius XI noted this fact decades ago: "We must never lose sight of the fact that the aim of the Church is to evangelize, not to civilize. If the Church civilizes, it does so through evangelization."[12] Evangelization operates more like a leaven within any culture that accepts the Christian message, the latter reinterpreting specific cultural traits.[13]

A passage of Paul VI's *Evangelii Nuntiandi* nicely sums up the task of evangelizing cultures: "For the Church it is not simply a matter of preaching the gospel message in ever wider geographical areas or to ever larger populations. It is also a matter of reaching and overturning, by the force of the gospel message, the criteria of judgment, the ruling values, the points of interest, the lines of thinking, the sources of inspiration, and the patterns of living among human beings that are contrary to God's message and salvation plan."[14]

FOSTERING HUMAN BETTERMENT

Depending on the time and place, the influence of the gospel message on cultures is exercised in many different ways and varying degrees of depth. In the strongest term it leads to a real "christianization of cultures," as was true in the past history of Europe. Then all institutions, philosophy, and law drew their inspiration from gospel principles. As we saw in chapter 2, Leo XIII frequently alluded to the Christian ideal that had shaped European societies over the centuries. John Paul II reaffirmed this historical fact in speaking to UNESCO. The whole of Europe, from the Atlantic Ocean to the Ural Mountains, "bears witness to the link between culture and Christianity, both in the history of each individual nation and in the history of the whole community."[15] Even today, the power of the gospel message is still capable of transforming the major cultural institutions of societal life: the family, education, law, work. But today the historical circumstances are different.

It would be a mistake to think that the Church wants to christianize societies by exercising cultural domination over them. As I noted in an earlier chapter,[16] Pius XII made clear that in modern society the Church works mainly through human consciences, trying to get individuals and institutions to freely accept such principles as are likely to promote justice, peace, and human dignity.

Thanks to Vatican II and its teachings, we have a better understanding of the different forms taken by the Church's work of evangelizing. We realize there are many different ministries and functions, due to the diversity of charisms. The mission of the Church is certainly carried out by the *witness of faith in Jesus Christ*, prayer, contemplation, liturgical worship, preaching, and catechesis. But, depending on circumstances, it can also take the form of dialogue with other believers, "to journey forward together in search of the truth and to cooperate in works of common interest." That would also include active *commitment to the defense and betterment of the human being, both individual and social*: a "real commitment to the service of human beings as well as any activity for societal improvement or against poverty and the structures that sustain it."[17]

Let us remember this important point: in a broader sense than the one we examined earlier in this chapter, the Church's work of evangelization is also carried out on the level of the *defense of the human being* and human rights. This will prove to be particularly timely and relevant in pluralistic societies and Non-Christian milieus, for example. Through dialogue and collaboration with all persons of good will, Christians, inspired by the gospel message, can engage in humanizing action to promote the integral development of the human being.[18]

When Christians join with other believers or persons of good will in serving human beings and their cultures, they perform an evangelizing action insofar as the gospel values concerning humanity and its dignity are defended and promoted. This aspect of Christian cultural action takes on considerable importance in an increasingly diversified and pluralistic world. We examined the import and scope of that task in the preceding chapters when we dealt with the defense of humankind and its cultural betterment. We also saw that the collaboration of Christians in the work of promoting justice finds its dynamism and motivation in their faith. In this sense, then, Christians can and must see that the defense of the human being as such ties in with a real gospel imperative of justice and charity.

METHODOLOGICAL POINTERS FOR THE EVANGELIZATION OF CULTURES

Right at the outset we must admit that there is no simple, agreed upon methodology to guide the evangelization of such an intangible reality as culture. But I do think that some *methodological pointers* can be gleaned from the Church's reflection and practice in this area.

1. The Church does not intend to work on cultures by way of authoritarian pronouncements. Its influence will be exerted by the active presence and witness of Christians, by encouragement, and by research.

2. Christians will have to undertake joint action if they want to have an impact on cultures. They must try especially to infuse Christian values into such *crucial cultural sectors* as the family, education, work, the media, health care, and justice for the most disadvantaged. They must also try to make sure that all segments of society share in the benefits of culture.

3. Broad freedom of evaluation and initiative is left to Christian communities in their concrete commitments to promote culture. The Church recognizes their proper realm of responsi-

bility, knowing that it is impossible to propose one way of thinking that would be valid for such a variety of situations. As Paul VI put it:

> In the face of such widely varying situations, it is certainly difficult for us to enunciate one way of thinking that will provide a suitable solution for all parts of the world. Indeed this is not our desire at all, even as it is not our duty. It is the obligation of Christian communities to scrutinize the true situation in their own region, to clarify it in the light of the gospel's unchanging words, and to derive principles of reflection, norms of judgment, and guidelines for action from the social doctrine of the Church as it has been worked out over the course of history.[19]

4. We must also acknowledge the fact that Christians, under the inspiration of their faith, may legitimately arrive at differing solutions with respect to socio-cultural issues. In such cases, as Vatican II pointed out, "no one has the right to appropriate the Church's authority for his or her opinion exclusively."[20]

5. In a pluralistic society especially, Christians are encouraged to undertake joint action in support of their cultural choices. But they must carefully differentiate their own initiatives from the Church's positions as such: "Let the faithful make a clear distinction between what a Christian conscience leads them to do in their own name as citizens, whether as individuals or groups, and what they do in the name of the Church and in union with its pastors."[21]

6. With each other, Christians are asked to make an honest effort at dialogue and mutual understanding in their commitments, remembering that "what unites them is stronger than what separates them."[22] Paul VI offered us the following principle: "In view of differing concrete situations and personal relationships, one must choose between the various legitimate pathways that lie open. The same identical Christian faith can lead persons to undertake different commitments."[23]

7. The evangelization of cultures calls for generous, ecumenical cooperation between all those who profess faith in Jesus Christ: "Catholics can cooperate with their separated brethren, according to the norms of the Decree on Ecumenism . . . in social and technical projects as well as in cultural and religious ones."[24] The desired cooperation should lead to a pooling of efforts that involves not only individual persons but also Church organisms.[25]

8.   One of the most difficult questions facing us is the question of socio-cultural change. Our efforts at evangelization must also deal with cultures *in the process of change and growth*. It certainly takes courage to face up to the *future of culture*. Christians must always seek a revitalized answer to the question that Christ posed to Peter: "And you, who do you say that I am?" Speaking at Laval University in Quebec, John Paul II noted that this question is of major importance for the future of the Church and the future of culture. Today culture is undergoing profound change. The culture that characterized a certain kind of Christendom has crumbled. Pluralism and materialistic values continue to progress, but so also does a new sensitivity for the promotion of the human being. A living culture certainly looks back at the past, but it also resolutely turns toward the future:

> Your culture is not just the reflection of what you are; it is also the crucible of what you will become. And so you will develop your culture in a dynamic, living way: full of hope, unafraid of difficult questions or new challenges, not allowing yourselves to be taken in by the glare of novelty and not permitting discontinuity or a void to creep in between the past and the future. In other words, you will develop your culture with discernment and prudence, with courage and critical-minded freedom vis-à-vis what may be called the "culture industry," and above all with the greatest concern for the truth.[26]

9.   It is important to underline the *freedom* that accompanies the activity of those who proclaim the gospel message and those who accept it. Evangelization must never be taken to mean a kind of collective indoctrination that is forced on a cultural milieu in an untimely or improper way. The power of the gospel message derives solely from the power of truth itself, which is capable of penetrating hearts and enlightening them as a light. This quality of freedom presupposes that the Church will have a profound respect for all cultures. By the same token, the Church is aware that by proclaiming such values as fellowship, justice, and dignity, it freely promotes human progress within all cultures. As John Paul II put it: "The Church respects all cultures. It does not impose its faith in Jesus Christ on any culture. But it invites all persons of good will to promote a true civilization of love grounded on the evangelical values of fellowship, justice, and dignity for all."[27]

10.   One final methodological pointer strikes me as being of particular importance. It is the need for joint research so that

we may better determine the situations we are to evangelize and discover the needed forms of collaboration. This topic will be the subject of the final section of this chapter.

COLLABORATION AND RESEARCH

Looking at the matter from a pastoral standpoint, we realize the necessity of a joint effort by all those responsible for Church action if we are going to infuse the spirit of the gospel message into a reality as pervasive and diffuse as culture.

John Paul II has called upon *episcopal conferences* to draw up adequate pastoral programs to deal with culture. They should enable local churches, in the light of the gospel message, "to confront the complex problems posed by the emergence of new cultures, the challenges of inculturation, new currents of thought, the sometimes conflict-ridden encounter between cultures, and the honest quest for dialogue between them and the Church."[28] In various regions the bishops have already appointed a relevant committee, an official, or even an auxiliary bishop to deal with cultural matters.

International Catholic organizations will play a major role in the coordinated activity of the Church in this area. They will serve as so many advance outposts "in the action taken by Catholics for the promotion of culture, education, and intercultural dialogue."[29]

Religious men and women also have an important mission to carry out with respect to cultures: "Many religious carry out important work in the realm of culture. More than one religious Order is dedicated to such activities as education, cultural betterment, and the understanding and evangelization of cultures."[30]

In short, if we are to evangelize cultures, we must first be able to *apprehend* the reality of culture as a field for Christian involvement and to *discern* which features of a culture are capable of ethical or spiritual progress and which run counter to the gospel message or even counter to human dignity. Pastoral work on cultures also calls for new *cooperation and coordination* between all those in charge of the Church's work in this area if they are to have an impact on widespread cultural currents that necessarily reach beyond the boundaries of one diocese or one country.

The whole Church must be sensitized to new mentalities that are tending to spread worldwide and penetrate all local cultures. Christians, lay persons in particular, must involve themselves in joint efforts to inject the spirit of the gospel message into the very heart of cultures. Such initiatives will be undertaken in a generous, ecumenical spirit that is respectful of the legitimate diversity of choices in an area as diversified as culture.[31]

All that will require a serious effort of *study and research* on the part of the universal Church. John Paul II had this to say to the Pontifical Council for Culture: "To you who have agreed to back up the Holy See in its universal mission to today's cultures I entrust the specific task of exploring and studying what the *evangelization of cultures* means today for the Church." And John Paul II made it clear that in-depth study would be necessary: "Through studies, meetings, group discussions, consultations, exchanges of information and experiences, and the cooperation of the many correspondents who have agreed to work with you in different parts of the world, you are hereby charged to shed light on these new dimensions with the aid of theological reflection, concrete experience, and the human sciences."[32]

At this point we can better appreciate what the present-day Church means by "the evangelization of cultures." Christian action on cultures is certainly not new in itself, but today it is rooted in a new and original approach to the modern world. John Paul II, in particular, has called attention to the new character of the Church's encounter with today's cultures. He discussed it in June 1980 when he addressed UNESCO, and he reiterated it in 1985 when he addressed representatives of the cultural world in Quito, Ecuador: "At the time of my visit to UNESCO, I wanted to lay the foundations for a new evangelization of the world of culture." When he created the Pontifical Council for Culture in 1982 his aim was "to lay the foundations for ongoing dialogue between faith and culture, between the Church and society."[33] His Quito address is important because he deals at length with the meaning that is to be given to the expression, "the evangelization of cultures," taking due account of all the essential and historical dimensions of the human being. In that address his focus is mainly on Latin America.

Indeed, the recent experience of Latin America has been a rich one and can be cited as an example here. After a period of slow maturation, the Latin American Church succeeded in formulating a concrete, realistic program at the Puebla Conference (1979) that offers much promise for the evangelization of culture in that continent. A few remarks here will serve to introduce this original Church initiative and perhaps prompt readers to consult the rich material to be found in the Puebla Final Document.

The "evangelization of culture" was one of the main themes discussed at the Puebla Conference by the bishops of Latin America, and John Paul II himself attended it. Culture is described as "the specific way in which human beings belonging to a given people cultivate their relationship with nature, with each other, and with God." It gives rise to a "shared lifestyle" and a "collective consciousness."[34] The common identity and cultural roots of the Latin American people lie in the shared substrate of Catholicism. The Catholic Church became the cultural matrix of their continent, where an Iberian population encountered indigenous Amerindian populations. This matrix produced a crossbreeding of peoples and past cultures profoundly marked by the gospel message. A faith of Iberian origin managed to undergo inculturation in indigenous milieus with their own rich religiosity. The challenge facing evangelization is knowing how to rely on this popular wisdom, a vital synthesis of diverse elements integrated by the Catholic faith, and preparing the cultural synthesis of tomorrow, one that will be receptive to the values of urban and industrial civilization in order to further the progress of Latin American peoples. New impetus must be given to a broad program of "participation and communion" in order to pave the way for the vital synthesis of tomorrow, one that will show respect for the Catholic cultural substrate and benefit the entire populace. In the process there is to be a "preferential option" for the poor, along with the young. The Catholicism of the common people "must be assumed, purified, completed, and reinvigorated by the gospel message." With regard to the future, the Puebla Final Document points out that "the Catholic wisdom of the common people is capable of fashioning a vital synthesis."[35]

On several of his trips to Latin America John Paul II dealt with the challenge embodied in the task of evangelizing the cultures of Latin America, whose history is so closely linked to that of the Church. Speaking to representatives of the cultural world in Ecuador, he pointed up the two complementary but dialectical aspects of this task: "In your nation the task of evangelizing culture entails two aspects. First, the mission of evangelization cannot be carried out on the margins of what is called to be your national culture. Secondly, the culture of Ecuador cannot, without betraying itself, fail to accept and welcome the religious and Christian values it bears within it. That calls for a fruitful interchange and an enrichment of those values." If such is to be the case, notes the pope, we must get beyond misunderstandings and suspicions:

Together let us build the road of truth which, being one, will ensure that the well-intentioned projects of all will converge toward it. Together let us build the civilization of human dignity, of incorruptible veneration for morality, of respect for the sincere conscience: in a word, the civilization of love.[36]

The next two chapters will attempt to explore this issue, the evangelization of cultures, in a deeper way by examining the approach now known as "inculturation." Chapter 7 will consider how the concept and methodology of inculturation have taken shape in the Church in recent years. Chapter 8 will attempt to survey the actual process of inculturation by considering the Church's encounter with various historical cultures. That will show us how the Church's dialogue with cultures, which was one of the main themes of Vatican II, has progressively made its way into the life of the Church.[37]

7/Inculturation: A New Concept of Evangelization

The term "inculturation" is a relatively new word in the official discourse of the Church. John Paul II is the first pope to use it; and he uses it frequently, as one can see from his talks during his four trips to Africa, for example. It is worth pointing out that some Christians were already using the term back in the 1930s, but it only gradually came into general usage. Vatican II did not use it, which is surprising when we consider that council's interest in the encounter between the Church and human cultures. Postconciliar study and research have contributed to its wider circulation, and the Jesuits have played a particularly important role in that process.[1]

These brief remarks, which I shall develop in the following pages, bear witness to a very illuminating evolution in the Church's recent experience. It is clear that the anthropological approach to problems of evangelization has become increasingly relevant and applicable. The Church has largely accepted the human sciences in its efforts to analyze cultural realities and to explore ways to practice evangelization.

Above and beyond the term "inculturation," it is the *process of inculturation* that we must understand and appreciate from a Christian viewpoint. We must try to pinpoint its dimensions, both anthropological and theological, traditional and innovative.

THE GOSPEL MESSAGE ADDRESSED TO EVERY CULTURE

Since its inception the Church's mission has taken the form of a mutually enriching encounter between evangelizers and cultures of the most diverse sort. St. Paul made Christ's message accessible to Greeks and other gentiles, and the gospel message was soon proclaimed in Rome and all the Roman and barbarian areas of the Roman empire. In later centuries theologians of genius, such as Origen and Augustine, sought to express the essentials of Jesus' message in the thought categories of the main cultures of their age. The whole history of the missions embodies an effort to adapt evangelization to the different languages, customs, and traditions of the countries that were to be evangelized.

So the effort to accommodate or interpret the gospel message in terms intelligible to every culture is not something new; it fits right in with Christ's own teaching, which was addressed "to all nations."

One of the earliest documents of the ancient Church depicts Christians as citizens completely adapted—today we would say acculturated—to the customs and usages of their milieu. They could hardly be differentiated from their compatriots, even though they called themselves "citizens of heaven":

> Christians are not differentiated from other human beings by their country, their language, or their customs. For they do not live in cities of their own, they do not speak any extraordinary dialect, and they do not practice any singular lifestyle. . . . They live in Greek and barbarian cities and follow the destiny of each. They conform to local customs in their food, their dress, and the rest of life, while manifesting the extraordinary and truly paradoxical norms of their way of life. As individuals, they reside in their own homeland, but as strangers who have taken up residence there. They perform all their duties as citizens and bear all the charges as aliens. Every foreign land is a homeland to them, and every homeland a foreign land. . . . They are in the flesh, but they do not live according to the flesh. They spend their lives on earth, but they are citizens of heaven. They obey the established laws, and their way of living is more perfect than those laws.[2]

The Church's directives for the first missionaries to Asia make clear that the task of the missionaries is not to carry France, Spain, or Italy to the new Churches. An instruction of the Congregation for the Propagation of the Faith dated 1659 deals with the practical issue of inculturation long before the term came into use:

> Do not offer any argument or exert any effort to convince those peoples to change their rites, customs, or ways unless those things obviously run counter to religion and morality. What could be more absurd than transplanting among the Chinese, France, Spain, Italy,

or some other country of Europe? Don't introduce our countries to them but rather the faith, a faith that does not reject or give offense to the rites or customs of any people so long as those rites and customs are not detestable, a faith that wants instead to see those rites and customs preserved and protected.[3]

The thinking of the modern Church on the encounter between the gospel message and human cultures took shape gradually. It developed mainly after World War I, which was when Benedict XV published his encyclical *Maximum Illud*. In that encyclical the pope first noted the work of eminent missionary precursors, who knew how to implant the Church in different parts of the world: Gregory in Armenia, Patrick in Ireland, Augustine among the Anglo-Saxons, Colomban among the Scots, Willibrod in Holland, Boniface among the Germans, Cyril and Methodius among the Slavs, Bartolomé de Las Casas in Latin America, and Francis Xavier in India and Japan. Then Benedict XV stressed that the planting of the Church in mission lands must take due account of the characteristics of the peoples in those lands. In a directive that would prove to be of great importance, he strongly encouraged the development of a native clergy, able to understand from the inside the people to be evangelized. The pope urged foreign missionaries to master the languages of the countries in which they labored so that they would be able to communicate with even the most educated persons. He also warned them to avoid any and all political or nationalistic designs. It sometimes happens, he noted, that some "subordinate the expression of the Church to patriotic aims."[4]

Pius XI took a close interest in the Church's activity during this new missionary era.[5] He, too, stressed the establishment of a native clergy. In mission lands young candidates must be solidly trained "not only to reach the priesthood but also to become teachers of the faith among their fellow countrymen." No distinction should be made between European and native missionaries. The latter are not to be considered mere aides but equals, some of whom will one day be able to exercise governing responsibilities in the Church. Missions cannot have any other aim but to establish and "naturalize the Church of Jesus Christ in those dearly beloved regions." Native priests understand, better than anyone else, the soul of their people, their customs, traditions, and language. Pius XI uses the very same arguments to advocate the training of native religious, both men and women; for it is especially through their involvement that the Church will be able to take solid root among their people. Pius XI also made clear how much this doctrine meant to him by increasing the appointment of native bishops and by backing the creation of seminaries, religious convents, and institutions of a charitable or educational nature.

Pius XII's appeal became even more earnest and urgent. For the twenty-fifth anniversary of Pius XI's encyclical, *Rerum Ecclesiae*, Pius XII issued his own encyclical, *Evangelii Praecones* (June 2, 1951). His message was clear and insistent. Future missionaries should not neglect anything in the way of training that would prepare them to understand the country in which they are going to labor. That might even include elements of medicine, agriculture, ethnography, history, and geography. Their aim is the spread of the faith and the establishment of a proper hierarchy. Like his two predecessors, Pius XII urged the training of a native clergy, and he formulated a basic principle of missionary adaptation: "We must follow the very prudent norm that when peoples embrace the gospel message, we should not ruin or destroy anything good, decent, and beautiful in their own character and native spirit." Every effort should be made to ensure that their arts, customs, and fund of knowledge are carried to a higher level of perfection. As early as his first encyclical, *Summi Pontificatus* (1939), Pius XII had committed the Church to gaining a deeper understanding of the institutions of various peoples and cultivating their best qualities and gifts: "Everything in the customs of peoples that is not inextricably bound up with superstition or error should be examined favorably and, if possible, preserved intact."

INCULTURATION AND ITS RELEVANCE TODAY

For reasons we shall be examining further on, the Church's encounter with cultures today is posing a new problem and arousing new interest. Progress in theology and the social sciences has enabled us to get a sharper focus on the crucial issue of "inculturation" and explore it more deeply.

The term "inculturation" is related to the term "acculturation." The latter term was first used by American anthropologists around the end of the last century; then it came to be used by German and other European anthropologists. In 1936 Robert Redfield and two colleagues offered an epoch-making definition of acculturation to their fellow anthropologists: "Acculturation comprehends those

phenomena which result when groups of individuals having different cultures come into continuous first-hand contact, with subsequent changes in the original cultural patterns of either or both
groups."[6]

The concept of "acculturation" has been employed for a long
time by Catholics in studying the relationship between the gospel
message and traditional or modern cultures.[7] It is still used by
Catholics; sometimes it serves as a synonym for "inculturation," as
certain discourses of John Paul II indicate.[8] But the tendency today
is to make a distinction between inculturation and acculturation in
order to make clear that relationships between the *gospel message*
and culture are not reducible to mere *relations between cultures* (i.e.,
acculturation). We are dealing specifically with the encounter of
the *Christian message* with cultures, and the term "inculturation"
suggests an analogy with the term "incarnation." The concept of
inculturation is not new,[9] nor can it be easily defined in a simple
formula. The complicated reality of this process is the object of
much continuing research by theologians and sociologists. Here
our aim is to understand the many dimensions of inculturation in
both theory and practice.

Let us start with a *working description* of inculturation as it is
generally conceived by Catholics. From the standpoint of the
evangelizer, inculturation is the effort to inject Christ's message
into a given socio-cultural milieu, thereby summoning that milieu
to grow in acordance with its own values so long as the latter can
be reconciled with the gospel message. Inculturation seeks to
naturalize the Church in every country, region, and social sector
while fully respecting the native genius and character of each
human collectivity. Thus, the term "inculturation" includes the
notions of growth and mutual enrichment for the persons and
groups involved in the encounter of the gospel message with a
social milieu.[10]

Inculturation applies first to individuals, groups, and institutions that incorporate gospel values. By extension it also applies to
the mentalities, customs, forms of expression, values, and practices that the work of evangelization is trying to reach. In this
chapter and the next I shall add further specifications and details to
this preliminary description of inculturation. The phenomenon or
concept of inculturation obviously does not signify a new reality.
But present-day happenings do give it a certain air of novelty.

The *present-day relevance* of the problem of inculturation for the
Church[11] is due mainly to the fact that cultural interchanges have

greatly intensified in our age, provoking confrontations between cultures and defense of popular cultural identity. The period of decolonization after World War II entailed a broad movement for "cultural" liberation and criticism of cultural dependence. In the young Churches of Africa and Asia, in particular, we see a historical reexamination of the evangelization effected by Westerners. They certainly managed to proclaim the Good News and implant the Church, but they did not always succeed in touching the innermost depths of native cultures. There has also been criticism of the methods of evangelization. Some critics do not hesitate to say that the attitudes of missionaries, seen *from a cultural standpoint*, was not wholly unlike that of the colonizers, administrators, and merchants who came to the new territories and *transplanted there the values of their mother country*. Europeans merely transferred their institutions, languages, practices, and ways of thinking from their home continent to another continent. Missionaries did announce Jesus Christ, but they kept thinking and operating within the cultural framework of their homeland.

At the time of decolonization, African and Asian theologians, and many Westerners as well, posed the issue of inculturation with new urgency. In particular, they wondered why local cultures had not been radically converted by Christian values in many instances, why a substrate of paganism continued to persist. On the other hand, missionaries had not always managed to perceive the religious possibilities of certain local customs. Theologians began asking how Christianity could become deeply inculturated in various cultures whose specific character was becoming better known and appreciated. They talked of stripping Christianity of its Western cultural dress in order to effect a real africanization, indianization, or indigenization of autochtonous Churches.

Debate about inculturation was not confined to the pastoral methods of the Church. It also dealt with the language of theology, moral teaching, and Church law, and with liturgical expression. Some questioners went even deeper and wondered how the Church might be able to welcome into its own inner life worthwhile elements of ancestral beliefs and ethical values espoused by traditional religions, perhaps even adopting their sacred texts. The seriousness and complexity of the questions raised in this debate pointed up the need for deeper studies of a systematic and interdisciplinary nature, studies that would pay respectful heed both to theological principles and serious anthropological analysis. The need was seen to determine some guiding criteria for the indispensable and complex task of inculturation.

CRITERIA UNDERLYING INCULTURATION

For the purposes of this present study, which is based primarily on Church documents, I shall focus on four criteria.

THE RADICAL DISTINCTION BETWEEN GOSPEL MESSAGE AND CULTURE

First, we must affirm the radical distinction between the gospel message and any culture. In other words, faith in Christ is not the *product* of any culture; its origin lies in a divine revelation. Furthermore, the Christian faith cannot be identified exclusively with any historical culture; such an identification would mean its dissolution. The heart of the Christian message surpasses and transcends every culture because it has to do with the revelation of the mystery of the incarnate and crucified God. St. Paul himself preached the radical distinction between this truth of faith and the cultures of his own day, the latter seeing only scandal or folly in his proclamation of the crucified Christ: "Jews demand signs and Greeks look for wisdom. But we preach Christ crucified, a stumbling block to Jews and an absurdity to Gentiles."[12]

John XXIII stated that it would be a mistake to identify the historical Church with Mediterranean culture, even though the Church saw the light of day there: "The Church does not identify itself with any one culture, not even with Western culture, to which it is linked by its history."[13]

The independence of the gospel message from any and every culure is ultimately rooted in the mystery of the Incarnation which, historically speaking, also includes the Crucifixion and the Resurrection. Here we are dealing with *divine facts* that transcend every civilization and every culture. It is in this context that we must grasp the exigency of inculturation for the Church. As John Paul II told the Biblical Commission: "The term 'acculturation' or 'inculturation' may well be new, but it perfectly expresses one of the elements of the great mystery of the Incarnation."[14] In one sense, inculturation prolongs the Incarnation in the history of human peoples.

Paul VI clearly spelled out the twofold principle that must be maintained in the process of inculturation. First, "the gospel message and therefore evangelization are not at all identified with culture. They are independent vis-à-vis all cultures." But once we have asserted this principle of *distinction*, we must not think that between the gospel message and cultures there is nothing but *separation or dissociation*. If that were the case, the gospel message could not possibly inspire cultures and transform them from within, as it has in fact done for two thousand years. Christ himself lived in a particular culture, and throughout its history the Church has become incarnate in specific socio-cultural milieus. Moreover, notes Paul VI, the gospel message is lived by human beings who are linked to their own cultures. And he adds: "The building of the kingdom of God cannot help but make use of cultural elements and human cultures. Although they are independent of cultures, the gospel message and evangelization are not necessarily incompatible with them; rather, they are capable of impregnating all cultures without becoming enslaved to any."[15]

This basic problem, the relationship of the faith to cultures, has been experienced since the very beginnings of the Church. Present-day thinking enables us to better understand the nature of Jesus' relationship with the culture of his milieu as well as the relations of the early Christian community with the Jewish community and with all Gentile cultures.[16]

PRESERVATION OF THE CHURCH'S IDENTITY

A second criterion is fidelity to the essential identity of Christianity as lived in the Church. The original teaching of the Church, its theological and moral doctrine, its pastoral and legal practice, and its liturgy have been enriched and deepened by generations of believers, pastors, thinkers, and saints. Their contributions are an integral part of the Christian heritage. It would be impossible to dissociate living Christianity from all the enrichment it has received from councils, the Fathers of the Church, and great theologians. They all have helped to bring the body of the Church to maturity. The Church would not be what it is without an Augustine, an Origen, an Athanasius, a Cyril, a Methodius, a Thomas Aquinas, a Francis Assisi, a Theresa of Avila.

Of course the Church of the past expressed itself in specific languages and in thought categories bound up with specific cultures; but recognition of such cultural interdependence does not nullify the perduring value and basic meaning of dogmatic formulations and ways of conceptualizing the faith, of basic sacramental and liturgical structures. The advances in theological reflection, biblical exegesis, the history of dogma, spiritual doctrines, conciliar and canonical formulations over the centuries are due to a maturation of the faith as it was lived in both the Eastern and Western Churches, parts of the universal Church. The Church of the future will continue to grow out of the same roots and the same common trunk that link it historically to its beginnings.

Thus, one of the primary laws of inculturation is to announce Christ to all cultures so that the Church may grow in them in acordance with its own proper nature and its own perduring identity. Inculturation, in other words, permits the Church to grow in every historical culture in accordance with the laws of its own proper growth. This is a point that must be clearly understood. The fundamental identity of the Church refers both to its *unity* and its *catholicity*. The Church's identity is not that of a uniform, undifferentiated system but rather than of a living body—that is, an organism composed of vital parts that contribute to the enrichment and unity of the entire body.

Vatican II clearly reaffirmed this organic conception of Church oneness. Indeed, the role of the Chair of Peter is precisely that of presiding over the "universal communion of charity," protecting all legitimate forms of variety in the Church and, at the same time, making sure that "particular elements serve unity rather than harm."[17]

In his talk to the Roman Curia on December 22,1984, John Paul II commented on this central passage of *Lumen Gentium*. He wished to show how the universal Church derives enrichment from the life of all the particular Churches and, indirectly, from all cultures, all nations, all languages, and all the achievements of human civilizations. Said John Paul II: "It would be difficult to express it more clearly or profoundly. The universal Church is presented as a *communion of Churches* [of particular Churches] and, indirectly, as a community of nations, languages, and cultures. Each of them contributes its own 'gifts' to the whole, as do every generation, every epoch, every scientific and social achievement, and every newly reached level of civilization."[18]

Thus, the identity of the Church presupposes a *communion* among all the particular Churches deriving their life from "the identical mystery of Christ." Each particular Church living in a specific culture must harmonize its *experience* with the experiences of all the Churches; otherwise, those experiences will not truly be "experiences of the Church," as John Paul II puts it.

Here we get the guiding principle for any and all inculturation, which seeks to promote the growth of one and the same Church within diverse cultures. Identicalness is not opposed to particularities; but it reveals its authenticity in the building up of *communion* and in the growth of the universal body of the Church. And that brings us to our third criterion: pluralism within the Church.

UNITY AND PLURALISM

A third criterion for inculturation has to do with the relationship between pluralism and unity in the Church. Safeguarding the identity of Christianity is in no way opposed to a healthy pluralism. Such pluralism has found expression in the particular Churches since the very beginning. Long ago the history of the Eastern Churches anticipated and embodied the pluralism that is now manifested in the concrete life of the Churches and the plurality of human cultures. Commemorating the fourth centenary of the Pontifical Greek College in Rome in 1977, Paul VI recalled that fact: "It is precisely in the Eastern Churches that we find anticipated and perfectly demonstrated the validity of the pluralistic scheme. Thus modern researchers, seeking to verify the relationships between gospel proclamation and human civilizations, between faith and culture, find in the history of those venerable Churches significant early elaborations of concepts and concrete forms directed to the binomial, *unity and diversity*." Paul VI went on to say that the Church "welcomes that sort of pluralism as an articulation of unity itself."[19]

Having clearly affirmed the adherence of ecclesial communities to this one communion in the faith, the Church unhesitatingly accepts a *pluralism* made up of discernment, fidelity, and ongoing investigation in the gospel encounter with cultures. On the one hand, as Paul VI noted, there must be fidelity to "the essential, identical . . . heritage, the selfsame doctrine of Christ, that is professed by the authentic, authoritative tradition of the one, true Church." But in the name of that very same fidelity we must be wise enough to discover new ways and expressions of evangelization. This calls for "deeper investigation of the cultural traditions of different populations, and of their underlying philosophical notions, in order to pinpoint those elements that are not in contradiction with the Christian religion or that can contribute to the enrichment of theological reflection."[20]

Unity is not uniformity. Paul VI expressed the Church's position in nuanced terms: "As I stated a year ago in Africa, if the Church is to be Catholic first and foremost, a pluralism of expression in the unity of substance is legitimate and even desirable when it comes to professing a common faith in one and the same Jesus Christ."[21]

The ultimate norm remains the *communion ecclesiae*, Church communion; and it holds true for all efforts to inculturate, adapt, or indigenize theology, Church discipline, and pastoral work. The rule laid down by Paul VI in the talk cited above is summed up in his phrase, "a pluralism of expression in the unity of substance."

In short, true pluralism is that which creates communion. On this point John Paul II reminded the Roman Curia of the thought of Vatican II, and specifically of its thinking in *Lumen Gentium* (n. 13). There the council noted that the universal Church is a communion of particular Churches. Comments John Paul II: "This [document] brings out the possibilities inherent in a healthy pluralism, but it also spells out very clearly its limits. True pluralism is never a divisive factor; it is something that helps to build unity in the universal communion of the Church."[22]

DISCERNMENT AND INVESTIGATION

The fourth criterion has to do with discernment, understood in the broadest sense and therefore including practical judgment and methodological reflection. For one thing, there must be deeper theological and anthropological investigation if we are to confidently promote mutual encounter between the faith and living cultures. As Vatican II pointed out, the particular Churches are also rooted in Christ and built up on the foundation of the Apostles and universal tradition. They must submit the teaching of the Church to "fresh scrutiny" and deeper exploration in order to discover, in the surrounding cultures, those elements that can be integrated into Christian living, Church discipline, and the liturgy, as well as to see how the faith can illuminate and enrich the native genius of each and every people. Vatican II suggests that in each major socio-cultural area theological reflection and investigation of this sort should be undertaken so that the young Churches may "take to themselves in a wonderful exchange all the riches of the nations that were given to Christ as an inheritance."[23]

This presupposes an ability to understand cultures and their potential receptivity to the gospel message. Attentive discernment is required. Insofar as indigenous cultures do not contradict gospel values, they should be welcomed with respect and preserved. Christians should reverently and gladly lay bare "the seeds of the Word that lie hidden in them."[24] What elements should be considered in this process of discernment? Vatican II says that we should focus respectful attention on a people's customs, traditions, sciences, arts, disciplines, view of life and the social order, and religious traditions. In areas that do not affect the faith or the welfare of the whole community, the Church has no desire to impose rigid uniformity. This holds true for the liturgy as well:

> Even in the liturgy, the Church has no wish to impose a rigid uniformity in matters which do not involve the faith or the good of the whole community. Rather, the Church respects and fosters the spiritual adornments and gifts of the various races and peoples. Anything in their way of life that is not indissolubly bound up with superstition and error is studied with sympathy and, if possible, preserved intact. Sometimes, in fact, the Church admits such things into the liturgy itself, as long as they harmonize with its true and authentic spirit.[25]

An attitude of respect and esteem for non-Christian religions will prove to be a fruitful means of inculturation. They are "living expressions of the soul of vast human groups" and echo "thousands of years of the search for God." They possess "an impressive heritage of profoundly religious texts." They all are sprinkled with countless "seeds of the Word" and can be an authentic "preparation for the gospel," to quote the fine phrase that Vatican II borrowed from Eusebius of Caesarea.[26]

If we base our efforts on the solid foundations of a theological discernment in order to promote a fruitful meeting between faith and cultures, we need not fear reductionism or confusion. Our efforts at inculturation will continue to enrich not only the local Churches but also the universal Church:

> Thus every appearance of syncretism and of false particularism can be excluded, and Christian life can be accommodated to the genius and the dispositions of each culture. Particular traditions, together with the individual heritage of each family of nations, can be illumined by the light of the gospel message and then taken up into Catholic unity.[27]

The particular Churches are historically identified "with the persons, but also with the riches and limitations, the ways of praying, loving, and viewing life and the world, that mark a given human ensemble." For them the task of inculturation is "to assimilate the essential core of the gospel message, transpose it, without any betrayal of its essential truth, into the language those human beings understand, and then proclaim it in that language."[28]

Inculturation essentially presupposes an attitude of receptivity and discernment. This is a complicated task. As Vatican II indicated, it calls for a serious effort of investigation in each of the major socio-cultural areas of the world.

NEW DIMENSIONS OF INCULTURATION

Concrete experience shows us that the actual work of inculturation takes on new dimensions that go beyond faith's relations with indigenous cultures. These cultures are no longer isolated, and they must now redefine themselves in the face of the spread of modern cultures to all regions of the world. The local Churches are faced with all the challenge of the newly developing nations, which are trying to preserve their cultural identity while opening up to modernization. I touched on these issues in chapter 4. The point to be recalled here is that *development* poses new problems both to the Church and to traditional cultures, and these problems cannot be disregarded when we talk of inculturation. The next chapter will enable us to examine the Church's experience in this matter.

We should also note that the work of inculturation also concerns the *traditional Churches*. They, too, face a real missionary task, as John Paul II has noted: "Henceforth the noble term 'mission' is applicable to the venerable civilizations marked by Christianity, which are now threatened by indifference, agnosticism, and even irreligion. Moreover, new sectors of culture are arising with diverse objectives, methods, and idioms. Thus, intercultural dialogue is imperative for Christians in every country." Only a real *quest for inculturation* will enable us to evangelize present-day psychologies and milieus, which means that inculturation must be "a long and courageous process."[29]

This poses an immense challenge to Christians in those countries that bear the historical imprint of Christianity. They must now engage in the difficult but stimulating task of a *second evangelization*. They will have to create ways for a new inculturation of the gospel message in cultures that are undergoing change and seeking their own deeper identity. This is the appeal that John Paul II unceasingly addresses to *Europe*; its Christian heritage should simultaneously inspire cultural renewal and spiritual renewal.[30]

A particularly complicated problem facing the Church today is the tendency in various milieus to reduce Christianity to social, political, or ideological dimensions. This tendency could be called the "culturalization" of the gospel message: that is, the exact opposite of inculturation. Today that phenomenon takes different forms.

THE CULTURALIZATION OF CHRISTIANITY AS A DANGER

In some Western countries secularization is eating away at Christian values and mores from within. In the collective conscience, Christianity is coming to be regarded as an established fact, as a cultural and historical phenomenon stripped of its radical meaning. Others see Christianity merely as a social entity whose political or economic importance is measured in terms of parties or interest groups. Christian dress still cloaks the language, institutions, calendar, customs, and feasts (especially Christmas and Easter) of a people, but all these values are mingled indiscriminately in the crucible of a pluralistic culture. Christians themselves are in danger of unwittingly adopting the judgmental criteria and behavior patterns of the vast majority. The gospel message is gradually losing its vital substance, even as salt loses its savor.

Given this situation, the task of inculturation is twofold: first, to perceive the danger of *reducing Christianity to something secular*; secondly, and even more importantly, *to proclaim the absolute of the gospel message*. This prophetic proclamation, then, must be a part of gospel inculturation; for the gospel message necessarily summons human beings to *break with* their contrary values and to *move beyond* their purely terrestrial interests.

As Paul VI pointed out, evangelization necessarily presupposes the proclamation of a "beyond," that is "the deeper, definitive vocation of the human being that is both in continuity and discontinuity with its present situation: beyond time and history, beyond the reality of this world and its passing form."[31] Christianity disavows itself when it offers an immanent salvation confined to earthly hopes. The Church does not preach merely an immanent salvation that is measured by material or even spiritual needs, confined to the boundaries of temporal existence, and totally identified with temporal desires, hopes, and affairs. It preaches "a salvation that goes beyond all those limits and finds its fulfillment in a communion with the sole absolute, God."[32]

INCULTURATION AND INTEGRAL LIBERATION

Another form of cultural reductionism threatening the gospel message comes from political and ideological movements that appeal to Christian values solely as determinants of their temporal activity. I am thinking of Christians who claim to be Marxist-Leninist militants in the name of the gospel message, or of those pursuing a policy of so-called national security who equate the gospel message with social conservatism. In the name of the gospel message, conservatives and progressists are clashing over the meaning of "liberation."

The relationship between evangelization and liberation is not a simple one. On the one hand, evangelization necessarily entails committed work for justice, as we saw in the preceding chapters. On the other hand, the fight for justice must avoid politicizing the gospel message, reducing it to an ideology of temporal struggle. Paul VI showed unusual vigor in reacting against this danger of reductionism. In a world seeking justice one may be greatly tempted to confuse the mission of the Church with the pursuit of a purely temporal project. Paul VI noted that many generous-hearted Christians, sensitized to the dramatic problem of liberation, were tending to reduce the mission of the Church to the dimensions of a merely temporal project or to purely political and social activity.[33]

Inculturation can be understood properly only if we have a correct understanding of evangelization. Evangelization certainly cannot be dissociated from the liberation of the human being, but it must take in the human being in all its dimensions, spiritual as well as material. That is required by the absolute of faith. It is the true liberation of the human being proclaimed by the gospel message: "It cannot be limited to the restricted confines of the economic, social, or cultural dimension. It must take in the whole human being in all its dimensions, including its openness to the absolute, even the absolute of God."[34]

The task of inculturation essentially presupposes a twofold fidelity: to particular cultures and to the universality of the gospel message. This tension is part and parcel of evangelization. Paul VI nicely summed up this dialectic of evangelization, which must simultaneously immerse itself in the concrete and preserve "its soul," its universal value:

> Evangelization loses much of its force and efficacy if it does not take into consideration the concrete people to whom it is addressed, if it does not use their language, signs, and symbols, if it does not

respond to their questions or link up with their concrete life. But on the other hand, evangelization is in danger of losing its soul and evaporating if it perverts its content under the pretext of translating it; if, in trying to adapt a universal reality to a local area, it sacrifices that reality and destroys the unity, without which there is no universality. Now only a Church that maintains awareness of its universality and demonstrates that it is, in fact, universal can have a message capable of being understood by all, above and beyond regional boundaries.[35]

The gospel message is destined for all peoples. It requires that evangelizers show profound respect for, and attention to, each and every human culture, so that they may perceive the highest aspirations of a culture and also summon it to transcend its own limitations.[36] At the heart of every culture we find a finiteness and a secret hope that also serve to reveal its capacity for transcendence.

The understanding and the practice of inculturation should be greatly encouraged by the document on *Faith and Inculturation* (1989) prepared by the International Theological Commission with the collaboration of the Pontifical Council for Culture (37). The document studies inculturation from the point of view of anthropology, theology, Christology, the Old Testament, the Apostolic Church; it then discusses such problems as: popular piety, relationship with non-Christian religions, the younger Churches, and the meeting of faith with the culture of modernity. The theological principle justifying inculturation rests in the Incarnation of Christ, as the document explains: "Because it was integral and concrete, the incarnation of the Son of God has been a cultural incarnation" (No. 12). Vatican II is quoted on that point: "Christ himself, by his incarnation, has been linked to the social and cultural conditions of those with whom he lived" (*Ad Gentes*, No. 10). The effect of incarnation continues, through history, and it tends to transform the whole of human reality expressed in the diversity of cultures. The document *Faith and Inculturation* says that "Christ would not reach us in the reality of our concrete humanity if he did not reach us in the diversity and complementarity of our cultures". This document, as noted John Paul II, should facilitate the understanding of Christian inculturation in its "biblical, historical, anthropological, ecclesial and missionary significance". John Paul II reaffirms that inculturation represents a decisive challenge for "the Church's action in the midst of traditional cultures as well as with the complex forms of modern culture". These theological orientations will now have to be translated into concrete programs of cultural evangelization (38).

The guidelines we have examined in this chapter become clearer and more precise when one considers the *Church's practice* in its encounter with cultures that are to be evangelized. The following chapter will describe some of the more typical experiences of inculturation to be found in today's world.

8/Concrete Experiences of Inculturation

In the life of institutions, events are often more eloquent than words. This holds true for the Church's *practice of inculturation*. Observing the behavior of the Church in the most diverse cultures helps us greatly to understand what the Church means by "inculturation." In this chapter I shall examine *concrete experiences* of inculturation in different parts of today's world: Africa, Asia, China, and India, in particular. I shall also consider inculturation in characteristic socio-cultural situations: among native peoples and refugees, and in multicultural societies.

On this matter it is indispensable for us to look to the actual *experience* of the Church if we want to see the rich and complex dimensions of inculturation. This is all the more necessary because there as yet is no official text of the Magisterium dealing methodically with the issue of inculturation in its entirety. It is by looking at the life of the Church in the most varied socio-cultural contexts that we come to grasp the scope and conditions of its works of inculturation. At the end of this chapter I shall try to briefly sum up *the lessons* of this experience.

THE AFRICANIZATION OF CHRISTIANITY

Paul VI was a true pioneer in boldly and lucidly broaching the problems of evangelization in modern Africa.

CATHOLIC FIDELITY AND AFRICAN EXPRESSION

As far back as 1969, when Paul VI was in Uganda, he spoke to the assembled bishops of Africa and laid down solid guidelines for

106

the work of inculturation on that continent. He told the Africans that henceforth they were to be their own missionaries, and he asked how the Church was to grow in Africa.[1] He focused on two points that clearly and firmly embody the guiding principles for all inculturation: *fidelity to the essential heritage* deriving from the Church of Christ and an *African expression* of that heritage so that a truly African Christianity could develop.

First, said Paul VI, your Church must be Catholic above all else—that is, "wholly grounded on one and the same identical, essential heritage, the teaching of Christ, that is professed by the authentic, authorized tradition of the one true Church." That means fidelity to the doctrine and deposit of faith in Christ and we cannot let other forms of religiousness supplant our adherence to the Church of Jesus Christ.

This first point calls for a second. Christianity must penetrate deeply into the native genius and culture of Africa, as a legitimate pluralism requires. Africans can and should have a Christianity that is African in its expression. This is the second principle of inculturation invoked by Paul VI: "The expression—that is, the language, the way of manifesting the one and only faith—can be manifold and therefore original, in line with the language, style, temperament, genius, and culture of those professing this one faith. In this respect a pluralism is legitimate and even desirable." Paul VI mentions the *domains* where inculturation is needed: the pastoral, ritual, educational, and spiritual domains. Thus, African culture will be the primary beneficiary of the riches that Christianity brings to all peoples and civilizations.

Pluralism is legitimate and desirable, said Paul VI, but there can be no healthy pluralism without *attentive discernment*. He did not hesitate to point out the dangers that may crop up, particularly when it is a matter of "religious pluralism." We must make sure that profession of the Christian faith does not become "a form of local folklore, exclusivist racism, egotistical tribalism, or arbitrary separatism." Grounded on a solid faith, Africans will not only avoid these pitfalls but also ensure that their growth as Christians brings enrichment to the universal Church: "You will be able to formulate Catholicism in terms that are completely suited to your culture and to offer the Catholic Church the precious and original contribution of 'negritude,' of which it has particular need at this point in history."

PROLONGATION OF THE MISSIONARY TASK

The broad lines of what Paul VI said in Uganda can be found in his message to Africa of October 29, 1967, *Africae terrarum*. In this important message he also elaborated a retrospective view of the work of missionaries in Africa. While acknowledging their limitations, he also underlined their undeniable merits in the work of evangelization. Paul VI readily admitted that missionaries may have failed to comprehend African ways and ancient traditions. They could not completely escape the mentality of their age, and they did not always manage to achieve an in-depth understanding of the customs and history of the peoples they were evangelizing. But the universal Church and the African Church must recognize and appreciate "their heroic undertaking." Their sole desire was to bring the gospel message to Africans: "Out of love for Christ, the missionaries left their family and homeland; and a large number of them sacrificed their lives for the good of Africa."

Paul VI reminds us that very often missionaries were pioneers bringing "the first forms of school education and health assistance, the first friendly contact with the rest of humanity, the first introduction to, and exploration of, knowledge data that are taken for granted today as elements of worldwide culture." Some missionaries did distinguished anthropological studies. The inculturation of the gospel message will now proceed by way of internal growth or *indigenization*, but that does not mean the end of all missionary aid from other Churches.[2]

Inculturation rightly lays stress on the *indigenization of local Churches* because Christians intimately familiar with a national culture will be the best evangelizers of their milieu. But indigenization cannot be set in opposition to *missionary work*. Native bishops are the first to condemn any hint of rejecting missionary cooperation. The bishops of Africa and Madagascar, for example, had this to say:

> We denounce, as contrary to the gospel message and the Church's authentic teaching, any and every act and spoken or written word that might hinder cooperation between the young Churches and the ancient Churches. This clear-cut stand on our part should suffice to rekindle the missionary impulse in generous souls who believe it is still possible today to serve the Church at home and abroad.[3]

Having said that, the bishops also point out that missionary activity should assume new forms in the future, forms that show respect for the legitimate autonomy of local Churches and their own proper responsibility.

We must also acknowledge the missionary work done by other Christian denominations. In fact, they are in friendly competition with Catholic missionaries insofar as they participate in the work of evangelization. Paul VI recognized the merits of both Catholic and non-Catholic missionaries. When he canonized the martyrs of Uganda on October 18, 1964, he said: "It was the White Fathers who introduced Catholicism into Uganda, preaching the gospel message in friendly competition with Anglican missionaries. As their reward for facing incalculable dangers and labors, they had the good fortune to be the educators in Christ of the martyrs whom we celebrate today as heroic brothers in the faith and patrons in the glory of heaven."[4]

GROWTH WITHIN THE CULTURE

Today the bishops and Christians of Africa are the ones continuing and extending the first efforts at evangelization. Speaking more specifically to African intellectuals, Paul VI said: "Africa needs you—your study, your research, your art, your teaching, not only for its past to be appreciated but also for its new culture to ripen on the ancient trunk and grow strong in the fruitful quest for truth. Faced with the technical and industrial growth that has reached your continent, your specific task is to ensure the vitality of the values of the human mind and spirit."[5]

The visible results of evangelization are the proof that Christianity has been solidly implanted in cultures. Addressing a symposium of the episcopal conferences of Africa and Madagascar in 1975, Paul VI took joy in the fact that Christianity had progressed so rapidly. A few decades had produced amazing results: a native episcopate, many vocations, vital communities, admirable catechists, and even the witness of humble Christians as martyrs. "Is not all that the mark of an authentic Christianity?"[6]

Inculturation does not mean a merely external adaptation of Christianity to a culture. It is from within that the gospel message must fecundate civilizations. Meeting the bishops of Africa on October 28, 1977, the tenth anniversary of his message *Africa Terrarum*, Paul VI spelled out this organic law: "The authentically Christian, Catholic faith must animate from within traditions and the civilization they entail. The Christian, Catholic faith has been grafted, as it were, on the venerable ancestral trunk; it is that faith which should give quality and savor to the fruits of the tree."[7]

Among the fruits to be expected from the Church's work in Africa is the transformation of societies in justice and peace. Through their sincere and generous commitment, Catholics make clear the renewing power of the gospel message and bear witness to the Church's unselfish service in African societies. Paul VI urges Africans to discover the Church's contribution to the cultures of Africa: "Don't be afraid of the Church. It honors you. It educates upright, loyal citizens for you. It does not foment rivalries or divisions. It seeks to promote healthy liberty, social justice, and peace. If it has any preference, it is for the education of children and the common people, for the needs of those who are suffering or abandoned."[8]

FULLY CHRISTIANS AND FULLY AFRICANS

John Paul II has reaffirmed and spelled out even more the Church's will to effectively carry on the work of inculturation in Africa. Addressing the bishops of Zaire and many other African bishops gathered in Kinshasa in 1980, he broached the problems of evangelization on that continent: "One of the aspects of this evangelization is the *inculturation* of the gospel message, the *africanization* of the Church. Several people have told me that it is a matter very close to your hearts, and rightly so. It is part of the indispensable efforts to incarnate the message of Christ."[9] The pope mentions some of the *areas* that deserve to be explored with a view to effective inculturation of the gospel message: the language that the Christian message should assume, catechesis, theological reflection, suitably adapted expressions of the liturgy and sacred art, and the communitarian forms of the Christian life.

Africans, he said, must be able to integrate elements deriving from different sources. Those sources would include the biblical culture, the historical cultures in which Christianity has matured over the centuries, and the new cultures to which the gospel message is addressed: "Last year, in my apostolic exhortation on catechetics, I myself called attention to the fact that the gospel message cannot be detached purely and simply from the bibilical culture in which it was first inserted, nor even, without serious losses, from the cultures in which it found expression over the centuries; and that, in addition, the power of the gospel message is transforming and regenerative everywhere."

In the area of catechetics John Paul II indicates that presentations should be adapted more to the African soul, while taking into account cultural interchanges with the rest of the world. In the area of liturgy he says: "A whole enrichment is possible, provided that the meaning of the Christian rite is well presereved at all times and that the universal, Catholic aspect of the Church (the 'substantial unity of the Roman Rite') shows up clearly, in union with the other local Churches and in accord with the Holy See." In the area of ethics a welcome must be extended to all the resources of the African soul that are so many stepping stones to Christianity. Africans must be able to discern what they are: "You know them better than anyone, those that have to do with the spiritual view of life, the sense of family, children, community life, and the like. As is true in every civilization, there are other features that are less favorable."[10]

On his third trip to Africa, in August 1985, John Paul II was even more explicit in encouraging "a tireless effort at inculturation."[11] He uses new and suggestive formulations to describe it. Inculturation is "the concrete form of the covenant between God and human beings in this time and place." Or, "it is the welcome acceptance of the universal truth by a human community endowed with its own specific sensibility and shaped by its own long quest for the meaning of life."[12]

John Paul II does not hesitate to specify the concrete *areas* where evangelization should bear its fruits: "daily life . . . mentalities . . . institutions." He spells this out in detail: the animation of rural and urban life, the improvement of crop yield, cooperation, literacy training, work among artisans, domestic training, the promotion of women, health education, housing, and the defense of right.[13]

The work of inculturation should take due account of the sometimes millenial experiences of traditional religions and customs. Prudent discernment is needed to retain what is sound and compatible with the Christian ideal, but also to break when necessary "with what is opposed to God's revelation" or with "what might be tainted with syncretistic practices." Moreover, Africans are trying to incorporate the achievements of modern civilizations. They are to do it with a moral freedom permitting them to avoid the materialistic mentality that often accompanies technological culture.[14]

The bolder inculturation seeks to be, the more it will presuppose serious searching and a sound spiritual formation. John Paul II reminds the bishops of Cameroon of this fact: "Hence the place that you will rightly give to the inculturation of the gospel message and dialogue between religions. As I explained to your intellectuals this afternoon, this presupposes a profoundly Christian and even theological formation to achieve fruitful results without losing Catholic identity."[15] Fortunately, that search is moving forward in Africa, both in the Church and in society. In that the pope sees a sign of hope for the mutual enrichment of cultures: "We must welcome as an opportunity the fact that we are seeing ongoing interchanges among intellectuals, scholars, social workers, economists, and spiritual authorities."[16]

The message of Paul VI and John Paul II is full of daring and discernment. The Church is making its own the cultural yearnings of the African continent. John Paul II acknowledges it in a phrase that reveals the full scope of the inculturation to be achieved. He urges Africans to be simultaneously "fully Christians and fully Africans."[17]

INCULTURATION IN ASIA

During the pontificates of Paul VI and John Paul II, the Holy See greatly increased its direct contacts with the Churches all over Asia. The Church has also spelled out its thinking on questions relating to the inculturation of the faith in these countries, which are so diverse in their traditions, languages, philosophies, civilizations, and religions.

HALF OF HUMANITY

The whole Church is becoming aware of the immense challenge embodied in the evangelization of Asia, where more than half of the human race lives. Paul VI was the first pope to travel through that vast continent. In 1970 he met with two hundred Asian bishops in Manila and said to them: "Young in its population but rich in civilizations that sometimes go back thousands of years, Asia is being driven by an irresistible will, as it were, to occupy its rightful place in the world;and its influence is, in fact, growing."[18] He identified himself with the Asian bishops, as with the successors of the Apostles, in the name of Christ's unique priesthood. The Church of Asia would have to find its own dynamics so that the faith might be inculturated there in an in-depth way: "No one can speak to an Asian better than an Asian can. No one should better know how to plumb the treasures of your cultures and come up with the elements to build in Asia a Church that is one and Catholic, that is grounded on the Apostles and yet diverse in its lifestyles."

In what fields might pastoral action engage to serve the faith and its inculturation in Asia? It can serve the faith "through catechetics, theology, education, the modern communications media, and ecumenical dialogue. . . . We cannot remain silent."

Furthermore, inculturation, or the "present-day adaptation of missionary activity," as Paul VI called it, entails courageous work on behalf of development. The pope who issued *Popolorum Progressio*, the great encyclical on development, was explicit, concrete, and insistent in urging Catholics to make a courageous social commitment.[19]

A few days later, again in Manila, Paul VI addressed himself "to the peoples of Asia." He expressed his admiration for that continent and its peoples: "We regard Asia with love and respect because of the venerable antiquity and richness of its millennial culture. This vast land has given birth to great civilizations. It has been the cradle of world religions, the source of a very ancient wisdom." Today, in a process of "mutual enrichment," those ancient currents are mingling with currents coming from the West.

Today Asia yearns for justice and the benefits of social and economic well-being; and it is struggling to overcome an incomplete development and unjust inequalities. Asia will be wise enough to find in itself the dynamism to grow spiritually while undergoing modernization: "We are especially impressed by the sense of spiritual values that dominates the thinking of your sages and the life of your peoples."

Relying on these spiritual values, Asians will be able to incorporate in a discerning way the technological, economic, and social advances to which their populations rightly aspire. Asians should welcome modern technological progress without succumbing to the peril of materialism. Their example could benefit all humanity: "Thanks to the spiritual vision you have received from your tradition, your sense of discipline and morality, and the integrity of your family life, you are certainly capable of opposing materialism; and you can even help Western civilization to surmount the dangers that besiege progress."

The Church respects traditions and wants to serve the progress of Asian human beings. One can recognize a connaturality between the East and the message of Christ: "Christ and his message certainly have a divine appeal that the profoundly religious East is capable of appreciating."[20]

INTERPENETRATION OF CULTURES AND THE FAITH

Inculturation entails an effort at indigenization that should now be undertaken by all Christians in lands that are to be evangelized. The goal is the interpenetration of cultures and Christianity, and this must first be achieved in the psychology of believers themselves. A couple of remarkable examples might be noted here.

In 1968, on the occasion of the beatification of the Korean martyrs, Paul VI marveled at the adaptation of Christianity to the traditional culture of that land. At the start the Koreans only had the temporary assistance of two Chinese priests, but they were marvelous at exploring their faith more deeply and identifying with it heart and soul. The Korean martyrs displayed a holiness that was in no way artificial or alien: "This holiness interpreted and carried to a sublime level the natural and spiritual predispositions of those obscure heroes, almost all of whom were lay persons barely initiated into the Christian life." Christianity transformed their psychology and their moral attitudes, but not by the importation of an alien culture: "It was a message cut to their measure and almost deliberately predisposed to enliven their natural gifts and awaken their best personal capabilities. Their Christianity was absolutely authentic and orthodox, and at the same time completely Korean." We see there a prophetic sign, as it were, "an inexplicable connaturality" between Korean culture and Christianity.[21]

In 1984 John Paul II urged Korean intellectuals and cultural figures to follow in the footsteps of their predecessors in the faith. The Church, he reminded them, "assumes everything in all peoples." Inculturation is a complicated task requiring *the collaboration of all*: "We face a long and important process of inculturation, so that the gospel message may penetrate deeply into the soul of living cultures. To encourage this process is to respond to the deeper aspirations of peoples and to help them enter the sphere of faith itself. Your ancestors, the first Korean Christians, saw this clearly."

The task of evangelization is twofold, said John Paul II: "To evangelize culture and to defend the human being." The Church and the gospel message are creators of culture through the Good News that is proclaimed. Often the heritage of the past is called into question, new currents of thought create confusion and divide generations, and the view of ethics is obscured by egotism and selfish interests. This is a challenge facing the Church in Korea, a country seeking modernization. The faith should inspire Koreans in all their efforts at modernization: education, research, literary and artistic creation.[22]

During his stay in that country, John Paul II proceeded to canonize the Korean martyrs. He again stressed the fact that those Christians had an admirable knack of inculturating their faith in their milieu. The Korean martyrs were the instruments of divine Providence in naturalizing Christianity in their homeland. They are the models to be followed today in attempting to spread the faith in modern Korea.[23]

On his trip through Asia, John Paul II stopped in Thailand. In Bangkok he described Thai culture as the product of an ancient wisdom drawn from Buddhism, in which all Thais see the roots of their culture and their identity. The Church can appreciate that rich tradition: "In the practice of Buddhism one can discern a noble inclination to make the effort to separate oneself from an 'earthly wisdom' in order to discover and achieve an interior purification and liberation. . . . The fruits of a 'peaceful and indulgent' wisdom are clearly evident in the Thai character. They are esteemed and respected by those who have the good fortune to meet you and to point out that this ancient wisdom could, if it opened itself to the gospel message, be enriched by the wisdom of the Beatitudes preached by Christ.[24]

We can see that the principles of inculturation expounded by John Paul II draw their inspiration from the teaching of Vatican II on non-Christian religions. Its guidelines are expressed by him in a cordial and concrete sense, due to the fact that he appeals directly and personally to the Christians of Asia, urging them to commit themselves to the promising task of inculturating their faith. He is the first pope to use the term "inculturation," it should be noted, and he uses it frequently.

THE ENCOUNTER WITH CHINESE CULTURE

To understand how the Church's effort at inculturation developed and grew, it is particularly instructive to observe the Holy See's attitude toward modern China.

Efforts at dialogue with China have noticeably increased since John Paul II became pope. The messages of the Holy See are particularly cordial. Addressing the Chinese community in Manila in 1981, John Paul II said: "Ever since divine Providence, in its mysterious ways, called me from my native land Poland to the see of Peter in Rome, I have ardently desired to express my affection and esteem for all my brothers and sisters of the Church in China."[25]

Every time John Paul II discusses relationships with China, he reserves a special place for the Church's dialogue with *Chinese culture*. The work and example of Father Matteo Ricci are cited frequently: "Matteo Ricci fully understood and appreciated Chinese culture from the very start, and his example should serve as an inspiration for many." John Paul II admits that not all have shown the same understanding. Some even opposed his work of inculturation. But that is past history: "Whatever difficulties may have occurred, they belong to the past. Now we must turn our attention to the future."[26]

The fourth centenary of Matteo Ricci's arrival in China was celebrated in 1982. John Paul II took advantage of the occasion to describe the work of inculturation done by that great missionary. From his studies at the Gregorian University Ricci received an education in the humanities, philosophy, theology, and the scientific knowledge of his time—disciplines that would prove to be valuable tools in his cultural contacts with Chinese civilization.[27] Matteo Ricci was one of the first to immerse himself in Chinese culture and society, while revealing the science and culture of Europe to that great people. He also introduced the cultural riches of the Chinese people to the West. He effected a real "cultural mediation," making himself Chinese with the Chinese and becoming another eminent scholar among the country's many scholars.

What must be underlined here is the long patience and detailed preparation that made Ricci's work possible. His apprenticeship took 24 years. He thus managed to become Chinese with the Chinese, to converse with them in their own language about the principles of morality in accordance with the tradition of Confucianism, and gradually to lead them to an understanding of the gospel message. He performed a seemingly impossible task, elaborating a Chinese vocabulary for theology and the liturgy. He thus created "the conditions to make Christ known and to incarnate the Church and the gospel message in the context of Chinese culture."

Another point of major importance is stressed by John Paul II: the inculturation that Ricci accomplished through the *personal witness* of his religious life. He knew how to cultivate the virtues that were especially appreciated by Chinese culture: amiability, affability, gentleness. "The inculturation effected by Matteo Ricci was not only in the realm of concepts and missionary work but also in the personal testimony of his own life." His work, said John Paul II, is comparable to that of the Church Fathers in an earlier day, who sought to reconcile the Church and Greek culture. What Ricci accomplished years ago remains valid today: "Between the Church and Chinese culture he managed to build a bridge that still appears solid and sound, despite the misunderstandings and difficulties that cropped up in the past and that still continue to crop up. I am convinced that the Church can steer toward this path with its eyes turned toward the future."

One aspect is especially spotlighted in John Paul II's message to China. Chinese culture and the Chinese nation are a unique reality, and there is no incompatibility between this people and the Church. On the contrary, there is the promise of a fruitful relationship for this ancient civilization as well as for the whole world. When the pope addresses Chinese Christians, wherever they live, he always refers to the one China that lies above and beyond the vicissitudes of history. Speaking to the bishops of Taiwan in 1984, he said: "You should be present at the core of all those values that form the culture of a people, those values in which a people recognizes itself as such above and beyond the momentary separations of history."[28] On the mainland of China there are other Chinese Christians, brothers and sisters in the faith, who lie hidden for the moment as so many seeds in the earth: "A day will come when Jesus can be transmitted and celebrated more visibly in the culture, the expectations, and the aspirations of the whole Chinese nation, which the Church respects and deeply loves."

The gospel message is addressed to Chinese culture as it is to every culture in the world. John Paul II reaffirmed this fact when he spoke to the Chinese community of Manila in 1981: "The Christian message is not the exclusive property of any particular group or race. It is addressed to each and every one; it is theirs. Hence there is no opposition or incompatibility between being truly Christian and truly Chinese at the same time." This means that Catholics can contribute fully to the construction of China. Catholics may work loyally for the progress of the country by respecting the traditional obligations of "filial piety toward parents, the family, and the country." Like all good Chinese, Catholics inspired by the gospel message "will cultivate the five major virtues—charity, justice, temperance, prudence, and fidelity."

There is a message of fellowship at the heart of Chinese culture and it links up with Jesus' message, which is a call to universal brotherhood: "Is it not thought-provoking to discover that a similar message can be found in your own Chinese maxim, 'between the four seas all humans are brothers'? More than ever we must proclaim that message throughout the world, where so much injustice and discrimination persists among peoples and nations."[29]

As we can see from the above remarks, the pope's message is addressed not only to Chinese Christians outside mainland China but also to the Church living as a "hidden seed" inside continental China. It also is addressed to all Chinese of good will, informing them of the Church's intention, prompted by gospel love, to serve "Chinese civilization and culture, which are among the most ancient and celebrated in the world."[30] So we see the Church patiently and hopefully expending more and more efforts at inculturation vis-à-vis modern China, as if history and actual experience were teaching it the modalities of evangelical dialogue.

THE RELIGIOUS AND CULTURAL WORLD OF INDIA

The promise and challenge of inculturation in India were vividly brought out during the truly historic trips of Paul VI and John Paul II. Both popes visited that land, with its unique treasury of religious and cultural traditions.

In December 1964, Paul VI seemed to be fascinated by India as it welcomed him with its cultural treasures and its potential for progress in the faith. He expressed his admiration for the Indian people: "For their innate nobility and for their artistic and cultural civilization, which reaches the highest peaks of the human spirit and on which the gospel truth can confer an unimaginable and universal plenitude and value."[31] The peoples of India are looking toward the future and social progress, and Christians are uniting with all the believers of India to ensure its complete development: "Are we not all united in the fight for a better world, in the effort to procure basic necessities for all, to fulfill a human destiny, and to live a life worthy of God's children?"

Paul VI cites the example of Gandhi. It will help to ensure the civic and moral virtues as well as the spirit of fraternal harmony that will enable the Indian people to be "an example for the whole world."

Proclaiming the gospel message in India, the Church has the greatest respect for the diverse beliefs and cultural characteristics of that land. It commits Christians to integrate themselves fully "into Indian civilization in an authentically Indian style." Heir to many cultures of East and West, the Church will again be enriched "by the contribution of its children in India, a contribution deriving from the precious and ancient cultural traditions of their country."

Noting the plurality of Christian traditions in India, Paul VI sees this as living testimony of the Catholicity of the Church. It "embraces all cultures; but at the same time it can express in a specific way the truth and beauty existing in each particular culture." Paul VI expresses his profound wonder at the unity of the Church, which is fleshed out in the diversity of human cultures: "Just thinking that people of different nationalities, languages, cultures, and lifestyles are called to be 'one single body and one single spirit in one single hope' fills us first with amazement akin to that of those who witnessed the miracle of tongues on the day of Pentecost."

The Catholicity of the Church should evoke in us "a greater desire for human fellowship and a need "to better know the peoples with whom we are making contact for the sake of the gospel message." We must try to discover their history and civilization, but also their "heritage of moral and religious values." Apostolic dialogue certainly rejects sycretism and irenics at any price, but it does not hesitate to recognize the authentic religious values of India even as the Church of an earlier day showed respect for pagans and gentiles. Adds Paul VI: 'St. Augustine was certainly strict when he affirmed the necessary relationship between the Church and salvation. But he also wrote: 'There can be no doubt that the gentiles, too, had their own prophets' (*Contra Faustum*, 19, 2: PL 42, 348)." The principle to be maintained in interreligious dialogue is that Christianity is not tied to any one civilization, but it is designed to be expressed "in the genius of every civilization, so long as the civilization is truly human and open to the voice of the spirit."

Note the richness and scope of Paul VI's words. They foreshadow positions that Vatican II would elaborate in its Decree on the Church's Missionary Activity, *Ad Gentes* (Dec. 7, 1965), and in its Declaration on the Relationship of the Church to non-Christian Religions, *Nostra Aetate* (Oct. 28, 1965). Paul VI's stay in India lasted only from December 2 to 5, 1964 and was limited to Bombay; but in itself it was a prophetic act because no pope before had undertaken such a trip. His apostolic pilgrimage and his talks made clear to the whole world the Church's burning desire for a closer encounter with the cultural and religious universe of India as that country was entering the modern age.

The bold gesture of Paul VI found a remarkable continuation in John Paul II's trip to India (Feb. 1–10, 1986). More than twenty years after Vatican II, a period during which pastors and researchers had forwarded reflections on inculturation, the pope traversed India and accorded a central place to gospel dialogue with India's religious culture. It is difficult to sum up briefly John Paul II's many statements on the subject, which show up right away as so many striking illustrations and deeper probings of Vatican II's teaching on the Church'c missionary activity and its dialogue with non-Christian religions. But I do think that the essentials of his message can be subsumed under four points.[32]

1. *The roots of Indian culture are religious.* John Paul II repeatedly expresses his profound esteem for the religious values of the Indian cultural heritage, which upholds the primacy of the Supreme Being and the priority of spiritual and moral values. We must recognize the truth of those spiritual realities, which transform the inner human being. The Holy Spirit is at work in every human being, and God is present in every person. God is equally present in human cultures, because God is the one who inspires the human being, the creator of culture. We must detect God's presence and activity in the heart of the great personalities who have enriched the traditions, institutions, and cultural heritage of India. John Paul II offers a particularly moving tribute to Gandhi. More than any other figure, he embodied the loftiest values of traditional and present-day India, and truly was "the father of the nation." Gandhi could rightly say: "The light that shone in this country was not on ordinary light."

2. *There must be further interreligious dialogue with India.* To meet India is to discover its religious traditions, and John Paul II stresses how important interreligious dialogue is to further mutual esteem, cooperative efforts in the service of humanity, and defense of the values shared by all believers. Those values would include God as the Absolute, the spiritual view of human life, and the ethical foundations of human living. This conviction leads us to see the human being as pilgrim on the way to the Absolute, a wayfarer journeying toward the contemplation of God. Culture thus takes on an eternal as well as a temporal dimension, and India offers a valuable spiritual contribution to a world threatened by the supremacy of materialistic values. Gandhi had set for himself the ideal of "seeing God face to face: I live . . . to reach that goal." It was the

secret of his activity in the service of India. All believers are called to come together and share their convictions about truths having to do with the Supreme Being, the spiritual destiny of humanity, and the personal commitment to foster the true elevation of human persons and human societies. The Church shows great respect for the religious traditions of India and the truths contained in them. This is what serves as the basis for sincere dialogue, for we are convinced that God's Spirit is at work in every human being. Speaking to representatives of non-Christian religions in Madras, John Paul II said:

> The Catholic Church recognizes the truths contained in the religious traditions of India. This recognition makes true dialogue possible . . . The approach of the Church to other religions is one of authentic respect. It seeks mutual collaboration with them, and its respect is twofold: respect for the human being in its search for answers to the most profound questions about its life; and respect for the activity of the Spirit in the human being.

3. *We must work for social and cultural development.* Believers of all religions must jointly confront the common task of building a more fraternal, just, and peaceful society in which all citizens, regardless of race, class, or religion, may be able to grow in accordance with their needs and talents. Education will play a role of major importance in this process. A new civilization is struggling to be born, a civilization that has respect for the culture of India, its embodiments in art, literature, and customs, and its openness to modern aspirations.

A month after his return from India, John Paul II came back to this common duty shared by all believers in a message sent to more than two hundred Christian university persons who were meeting in Bangalore: "Dialogue, understanding, and cooperation among all religions should be the permanent concern of educators and religious leaders, in order to ensure the progress of culture, justice, peace, and fraternity. Thus culture becomes the common ground of our service to the cause of humanity."[33] That had been Gandhi's appeal to his brothers and sisters: "Overcome hatred by love, lying by truth, violence by suffering." John Paul II invokes the law of toleration in the Indian constitution and calls for the construction of a civilization of love and justice, a civilization that will allow for every legitimate form of diversity framed in the harmony of peaceful dialogue.

4. *We must promote the inculturation of the gospel message.* To achieve

its full flowering, any and every culture must accept God, who satisfies the human being's thirst for the Absolute. The Church respectfully addresses Indian culture, which already welcomes the Supreme Being and has been sensitized to spiritual values by asceticism and renunciation, and it tells that culture that God has been fully revealed in Jesus Christ. To transmit the gospel message, the Church proposes a salvation dialogue—that is, a form of inculturation that dovetails with the native spirit and soul of each people and shows respect for all that is true, beautiful, and good therein. That is how the Church operates in India. It is enriched by those values in India insofar as it accepts and elevates them in Christ. The local Churches, pastors in particular, have the responsibility of fostering this inculturation through a process of discernment involving assiduous prayer and research. In communion with the universal Church, this will ensure a fruitful interchange between the gospel message and the traditional wisdom of the people as well as a thoroughgoing incarnation of the life of faith in the mentality of Indian culture. Bishops have a specific duty in this matter, particularly with respect to the "inculturation of the liturgy," which always presupposes "doctrinal verification" and the "pastoral preparation of the faithful." For their part, lay persons will involve themselves in their own proper spheres of action: economics, politics, societal life, cultural affairs, the arts and sciences, international life, and the media. Divine revelation is intended for the noble civilization of India as the fullness of hope in its encounter with the living God.

Readers can see that inculturation presupposes familiarity with everything true and beautiful in the Indian spirit so that its response to Christ's summons may move it beyond its own limitations and elevate its own culture to enrich the whole Church. Remaining faithful to itself, Christianity must become Indian with the people of India. Speaking to young people in Bombay, John Paul II summed up inculturation this way: "For you believe in him, Jesus Christ has become Indian."

INCULTURATION AND CULTURAL DIVERSITIES

The Church's encounter with cultures takes many forms because the surrounding conditions vary as much as do the cultures that are to be evangelized. In an earlier day inculturation may have been seen as the insertion of the Church into homogeneous cultures. Today, in the light of concrete experience, we are duly aware of the many different subgroups or subcultures that the Church must reach. On his many trips John Paul II has been prompted to broach this very complicated aspect of inculturation. I shall consider a few examples here: the culture of *indigenous peoples* living in countries that are part of Western civilization; the problem of *refugees* living among populations with alien cultures; and the problem of *multicultural societies*, which can be found both in highly industrialized societies and in developing nations. Let us see how the Church proposes to approach the inculturation of these different milieus.

THE CULTURE OF INDIGENOUS PEOPLES

On several of his trips to Latin America and North America, John Paul II has paid particular attention to the situation of *indigenous peoples*. Addressing the Amerindians of Canada, he recalled a document issued centuries ago by Paul V, *Pastorale Ufficium* (1537). That document had proclaimed the rigths of native populations and defended both their freedom and their particular characteristics. John Paul II reminded the Amerindians of Canada that Christianity came to meet them, thanks to Roman Catholic missio-. naries and missionaries of other Christian denominations. They tried to be like the native Amerindians in order to serve them and bring them the gospel message. There may well have been misunderstandings and mistakes in their work, and John Paul II forthrightly states that the Church is prepared to make up for the unintended wrongs resulting from their actions: "Whatever may have been their faults and imperfections, whatever mistakes they may have made, whatever wrongs may have unintentionally resulted, they are now trying to make up for them." The missionaries remain your best friends, says John Paul II to the Amerindians. It was thanks to them that "education and health care have managed to take shape, and the Grey Sisters have made an admirable contribution in those areas." Going further, the pope reminds the Amerindians that if a *cultural revival* is now under way among them, it is in large part due to the linguistic and anthropological studies that the missionaries managed to pursue. The Church has become the advocate of their cultures, their rights, and their heritage.

The native ethnic groups represent a great diversity of cultures and religious traditions, but their mutual cooperation "is a sign of hope for building solidarity among the country's aborigines." History tells us that in the past their cultures were disregarded and even despised. Today, fortunately, that situation has been largely reversed. People are now learning "to recognize the great richness of your culture and to treat you with greater respect." John Paul II vigorously denounces every form of oppression: "I also condemn any and all physical, cultural, and religious oppression, as well as anything that would deprive you of what is legitimately yours."

Certain consequences should flow from their rights. The first is "a fair measure of self-determination in your lives as native peoples." The Church is happy to know that negotiations over this matter are in progress. It invites the native peoples, in turn, to put their talents in the service of others for the common welfare of Canada and "to build a civilization of justice and more authentic love."[34]

We find similar points made by John Paul II in his meetings with other native peoples in other countries: for example, in the United States, in Brazil and other nations of Latin America. One of his most important addresses on the culture of native peoples in Latin America is the one he gave in Ecuador in 1985. Addressing more than a hundred thousand Amerindians of various tribes, he vigorously defended their dignity, their cultural traditions, and their right to complete self-development along with the descendants of all the nation's communities: "Your dignity is not inferior to that of any other person or race." Their age-old culture, he said, contained "seeds of the Word" even before evangelization came. He cites several features of their traditions: their sense of life and death, their sense of justice, the value placed on their word, their high regard for mutual relationships between human beings. These values find their fulfillment in the gospel message: "From the very beginning, without you realizing it, your heart sensed God's great desire that all races and cultures unite in a single community of love, in one immense family whose head is Jesus."

John Paul II encouraged them to reconcile their desire for cultural fidelity with their yearning for modern development. "For centuries your community has been committed to preserving its values and its culture." Today they are joining the larger community, which will allow for "the development of your culture" and enable it to assimilate "the discoveries of science and technology in its own proper way." It is perfectly legitimate for them to want to preserve the spirit of their cultures, but one precondition must be met if their rights are to be protected: "Your culture is bound up with real, effective possesion of land." Hence all efforts by government and the Church to achieve a just agrarian reform must be encouraged.

Adverting specifically to the task of evangelization as such, John Paul II says that we do not do violence to cultures by proclaiming to them the true God and Christian principles. He cites the Puebla Final Document (n. 406): "We see nothing violent in the fact that evangelization invites peoples to abandon false conceptions of God, anti-natural patterns of conduct, and aberrant manipulations of some people by others." The Church has every intention of respecting all that is valid in cultures; but its mission is "to raise customs to a higher level by preaching the morality of the decalogue, the most basic expression of human ethics that was revealed by God and brought to complete perfection by the law of love that Christ taught." John Paul II tells them affectionately:

> You have a place reserved for you in the Church. Blessed will be the day when your own Christian communities can be served by missionary men and women, priests, and bishops of your own stock. Then you and your brethren belonging to other peoples will be able to worship the one true God, each according to its own proper characteristics but all united in the same faith and love.[35]

REFUGEES AND THEIR CULTURE

In its work of inculturation the Church confronts a dramatic and extreme situation when it encounters refugees. Today there are more than twelve million refugees living in pitiful situations of physical and cultural poverty. When he went to Bangkok, John Paul II dwelt at lenght on the refugee problem. Addressing refugees themselves, he told them of the Church's love for them: "Hear these words that well up from my heart. I want you to know that I love you. We are truly brothers and sisters, members of the same human family, sons and daughters of the same Father who loves us. I want to share your sufferings, your difficulties, your pain so that you may know that someone loves you, takes pity on your plight, and is trying to help you find solace, comfort, and a reason for hope." Speaking later to government representatives and the diplomatic corps, the pope stressed the physical and cultural humiliation of refugees, who arrive completely empty-handed: "They are in a state of total dependence on others for their food, clothing, housing, and every decision regarding their future. . . . These many victims suffer a truly cruel misfortune. Unable to return to their own country, they cannot remain indefinitely in their present situation." Their difficulties are not solely of "a material nature." Their basic physical needs must be met, of course, but they must also be provided with education, helped to preserve their cultural identity, and offered moral and psychological support. It is not enough merely to transport them from one place to another: "They have *the right to return to their roots*, their native land, with its rights to national sovereignty, independence, and self-determination. They are entitled to all the cultural and spiritual relationships that nourish and sustain them as human beings."[36]

The problems of refugees are often linked up with the violence oppressing races, tribes, and ethnic groups. Paul VI and John Paul II have had the courage to denounce the crimes committed against justice and human cultures in the conflict of tribes and races. In 1980 John Paul II addressed the diplomatic corps in Nairobi, Kenya. He reminded them of what Paul VI had said in his last address to the diplomatic corps. Paul VI had expressed the Church's deep concern over "the intensification of racial and tribal rivalries and the consequent increase of rancor and divisiveness." He had denounced "the attempt to create juridical and political structures that, violate the principles of universal suffrage and popular self-determination."[37] One of the most violent forms of racial and cultural oppression is *apartheid*, which deprives ethnic groups of their freedom of movement and political activity in their own native country. John Paul II has bluntly denounced this form of violence: "It is deplorable to see the continued existence of an *apartheid* system which, by harsh repression, continues to pile up victims and trample underfoot a basic human right."[38]

John Paul II established a direct link between racist oppression and the phenomenon of migration. Racial discrimination drives the rural masses to cities, artificial centers of segregation, or foreign countries; it seriously damages countless men and women and violates their dignity. These human beings are deprived of their rights, their due to liberty, their dignity, and their culture. The international community and all nations are urged to make sure that within their own boundaries "a just liberty is offered to all citizens so that none of them are obliged to go looking for it elsewhere."[39]

The pope notes the praiseworthy efforts of Christian groups who identify with refugees to bring them the solace of fellowship and defend their cause in the international arena. The Church's witness among these millions of refugees takes the form of love, first of all "I want you to know that I love you," said John Paul II—because these poorest of the poor are in danger of being forgotten and abandoned by world opinion. In the name of the gospel message we must denounce this intolerable situation and mobilize all human beings of good will to liberate refugees from the political, physical, and cultural violence that is imposed on them. The Church's work among these groups is difficult and very complicated because refugee groups include persons from a wide range of social and cultural circumstances: illiterate persons on the one hand, university persons on the other. With respect to refugees themselves, there is a need to assuage their immediate miseries, educate their children, and hasten their return to a decent political and cultural situation.

Such are the guidelines for the Church's work in this abnormal situation that affects more than twelve million persons and tends, alas, to be self-perpetuating. It is an enormous challenge for Christians to confront such a socio-cultural milieu, try to understand it, and inject into it the gospel hope of justice and fellowship. It is one of the most complicated forms of inculturation that we must practice today.

MULTICULTURAL SOCIETIES

We shall now consider another situation: the Church's encounter with societies that contain a multiplicity of cultures. To men and women living in *multicultural* societies, where we find cultural, racial, and linguistic pluralism, the Church wishes that the gospel message become a source of mutual understanding and participation in the common welfare. John Paul II stressed this point in speaking to the multicultural population of Canada: "The gospel message has been, and ever continues to be, a source of spiritual culture for men and women of diverse nations, languages, and races." He applied the principle to Canada: "This statement is particularly meaningful for Canada, where the varied heritage of peoples, nations, and cultures, due to immigration, constitutes the common good of the whole society."

If that harmony is to be reached, however, there is an indispensable precondition. The culture of each specific group must be inspired by the gospel message of love: "If you dissociate your culture from its ties with the gospel commandment of love, the multicultural relationships characteristic of Canada will be rendered impossible." John Paul II points out that the vitality of Canada is due to the collaboration of its two founding peoples, the French and the English. Respect for their own cultural identity has enabled them to have respect for the many diverse immigrant populations from Europe, Asia, and Latin America. Harmony and unity can be built amid much diversity for the benefit of the whole collectivity: "Pluralism in traditions, cultures, histories, and national identities is compatible with societal unity." The underlying inspiration and principle must be a combination of mutual understanding and love. Several times in that address John Paul II alluded to a "civilization of love." He wanted to see Canada become "a civilization of durable love" that would guarantee "the priority of ethics over technology, the primacy of persons over things, and the superiority of spirit over matter."[40]

The Church's encounter with multiracial and multicultural societies compels us to broaden what could be a narrow, unilinear view of inculturation. Some countries (in Asia, Africa, and Latin America, for example) contain ethnic groups that differ from each other a great deal. Some national Churches contain hundreds of ethnic groups, each with its own language and culture. In such places the whole task of inculturation is extremely complicated, as John Paul II noted during his trip to Papua. He stressed the peculiar conditions of that country, where so many different cultures and traditions live side by side. This calls for a wholly original approach by the Church in its efforts at inculturation. As John Paul II said to the bishops of Papua New Guinea and the Solomon Islands: "The Holy Spirit has given the Church in your country unity in diversity. The faithful belong to many different cultures and traditions, as we see from their many different languages and customs." Missionaries themselves come from many countries and religious orders. The dioceses differ in their historical development. Yet, amid such great diversity, all are one in faith, hope, and charity.[41]

Today the phenomenon of multiculturalism is attracting the attention of evangelizers in many parts of the world. *The Church in the United States* learned long ago how to face up to a multiplicity of races, languages, and cultures.[42]

The second visit of John Paul II to the United States (September 10–19, 1987), a country with hundreds of cultures and subcultures and regarded as the most heterogeneous nation in the world—in fact, as a cultural cross section of the world—was an unusual opportunity for the pope to give special attention to a favorite theme of his, the *evangelization of cultures* and *inculturation*.

Going through the fifty discourses that he delivered during his ten-day visit to the United States, one is struck again and again by his sensitivity to the uniqueness of the American cultural scene. Meant is his sensitivity to the presence of: a *dominant* distinctly and thoroughly pluralistic U.S. culture, numerous *subcultures* that are closely related to this dominant culture, and the many more or less independently functioning *minority cultures*. One could hardly wish for a better setting to illustrate what is meant by *inculturation* and *the evangelization of cultures*.

One is struck also by the Holy Father's constant awareness of how particular Churches, and he as Chief Shepherd of them all, must keep in mind three distinct responsibilities when dealing with the challenge of inculturation. 1) The Church must respect *all* cultures and subcultures. *Every* cultural group, whether large or small, has a Godgiven right, as far as possible and feasible, to express its faith in terms of its own "soul", in terms of its own ways, traditions, basic assumptions, attitudes and goal, and identity. 2) The Church must *positively encourage* (not merely tolerate) inculturation. A Christian community is, in fact, never so authentic as when it expresses its faith in terms of its own innermost self, and therefore in terms of its own culture. 3) The particular Churches and their Chief Shepherd have at the same time an important *prophetic* role to play: at times they must be *countercultural*.

These principles were clearly evident in all the pope's homilies, talks, and exchanges with the American hierarchy, priests, religious, and laity.

The location for the various discourses and exchanges had been very carefully planned, so that the special cultural character of the city or state would correspond to the issue discussed. Thus challenges facing the *dominant* American culture were of primary concern at the pope's first stop (Miami), at the meeting with the President of the United States, and especially in the exchanges that took place with the hierarchy, priests, religious, and laity. The special needs of *subcultures* and *independent minority* cultures were discussed, for example: in Miami, "the crossroad of cultures"; in New Orleans, the heart of the Black South and the home of the only Black Catholic university; in San Antonio and in the various cities of California, the home of millions of Hispanics and Asiatics; and in New Mexico, Arizona and California, the home of the American indigenous peoples. Some meetings were held in locations that represented special concerns or a special potential for evangelization, e.g., California as a center of communication and technology and the new home for many migrant farmers and refugees.

Today the Church in the United States is making a specific effort to meet populations of Hispanic language and culture, whose numbers have greatly increased because of immigration and natural increase. The United States Church is being obliged to adapt its pastoral work to the needs of Hispanic communities and to send them adequately trained educators, priests, and bishops.

In *Western Europe* there has been a noticeable increase in the mingling and confrontation of cultures in recent years, due to the arrival of large numbers of foreign workers and to much immigration. The local Church must learn to dialogue not only with European immigrants but also with large communities of Muslims, Africans, and Asians. The Church faces a major challenge in its task of evangelization. It must find new ways to promote the inculturation of the faith among these newly arrived populations.

As we saw above, multiculturalism is a constant in the work of evangelization being carried out in Africa. As John Paul II said in Cameroon, some African countries are veritable crossroads "of ethnic groups, languages, and religions."[43] In them the work of inculturation can never be limited to one single culture.

We find a similar situation in many parts of *Latin America*. In Ecuador, for example, John Paul II addressed more than a hundred thousand Amerindians belonging to at least twenty different ethnic groups. He noted that missionaries in Ecuador must be given credit for dedicating themselves totally to those groups in order to comprehend their languages and cultures, and to bring faith in Jesus Christ to them. Today the Church is helping these ethnic groups to open up to the benefits of modern civilization while safeguarding the richness of their own cultures.[44]

A serious problem now pressing its attention on the Church in many countries is the *mass migration* of populations of diverse races and cultures. It is a problem faced on several continents. The Pontifical Council for the Pastoral Care of Migrants and Tourists has done much to make the whole Church aware of these problems.[45]

Thus, in various regions of the world, the Church is engaged in patient *multicultural dialogue*. Concrete experience brings out clearly the preconditions for fruitful inculturation: respectful attention to the diversity of cultures; the need for intercultural understanding; the need for close cooperation among all evangelizers; finally and most importantly, ongoing insistence on the goal of evangelization, which is to build up the universal communion of faith in Christ in and through the multiplicity of its human expressions.

THE LESSONS OF EXPERIENCE AND INCULTURATION

As I come to the end of these two chapters on inculturation, I should like to sum up briefly the points that seem most important for further reflection on the subject. I leave it to the theologians and sociologists to pursue their work of systematization and I simply offer a few main points in a series of propositions.

1. Inculturation, the basic effort to adapt the work of evangelization, is not new. But the concept has taken on a certain novelty, due to a characteristic development of our own age: the affirmation of cultural identities on the one hand, and on the other hand the reawakened attention of pastors and theologians to everything relating to the Church's incarnation in diverse cultures.

2. Inculturation directly has to do with the countries or regions that are to be evangelized with due respect for their characteristic traditions and cultures. But it also takes in such psycho-social phenomena as behavior patterns, customs, traditions, and mentalities. Thus, the gospel message must be inculturated in *psychological* territory as well as in *geographical* territory. In other words, it must also link up with the ways of thinking, judging, and acting that characterize human collectivities.

3. Given the ongoing growth of pluralism, the task of inculturation must often confront a situation of *cultural plurality*. Such is the case, for example, when the very same territory is inhabited by different ethnic communites, majority and minority groups, migrants, refugees, transient populations, or displaced persons.

4. Inculturation implies and entails respect for two basic realities: the *gospel's essential message*, which is a basic, irreducible, and original datum form the outset; and respectful openness to *all the cultures* to which the gospel message is addressed. Let us also note that inculturation involves the evangelizers as well as those to be evengelized because the evangelizers, too, share historically in a specific culture and must enter into creative dialogue with the culture of those who open themselves to Christ and the Gospel message.

5. Inculturation benefits the *local Churches* and the *universal Church*. Indeed, the Church is all the more *Catholic* insofar as it is more deeply implanted in the heart of a given culture, in time and space. The whole Church is enriched by the contributions of each culture, and each culture grows by sharing in the richness of the *communio ecclesiae*.

6. The task of inculturation entails the insertion of the gospel message into a culture at *every level of Church activity*: the language of preaching and the expression of the gospel message in catechetics, theological research, the liturgy, sacred art, community living, ecumenical dialogue,and charitable service.[46] Hence the task of inculturation calls for *close cooperation and coordination* among all those responsible for evangelization. The witness of Christian living effectively contributes to the inculturation of the gospel message in a milieu.

7. Inculturation also entails committed work on behalf of *justice, development*, and the *betterment of the human being*. This is an obligatory feature of the work of evangelization. The inculturation of the gospel message should lead people to a sense of justice, peace, and solidarity. This goal is pursued by teaching the social principles of the gospel message and commitment to the promotion of justice. Here lay persons have an indispensable role.

8. Inculturation does not apply solely to the traditional or present cast of cultures. It also applies to the *ongoing growth or development of cultures*, to newly emerging values that await the enrichment which the gospel message can provide. This holds true for newly created nations and for the already industrialized nations, because cultural changes are taking place everywhere and transforming lifestyles and institutions. In actual practice inculturation is a never-ending process because the Church must accompany cultures through their whole process of growth and development. Special attention must be paid, however, to newly created nations and the younger generations.

9. In the Church's encounter with non-Christian religions, inculturation hinges on three essential points of dialogue. First, the *Christians message* must be proclaimed. Second, the values of *traditional religions* must be discovered. Third, and this is becoming increasingly important in our age, we must be attentive to the worldwide spread of *modern values*. Christians can do fruitful evangelization work by reflecting with non-Christians on the proper way to give a discerning reception to the values of technological society, values that are now spreading to all peoples.

10. If inculturation is not to become mere accomodation to cultures, a twofold basic attitude and approach is required. It is a compound of *theological discernment* and *anthropological perceptiveness*. On the one hand, inculturation must be grounded on the *identicalness* of one and the same traditional faith so as to simultaneously ensure the catholicity of the Christian creed and pluralism in its theological expression. On the other hand, we must be capable of perceiving all the values and expectations of a culture that can be reconciled with the gospel message, if faith is to penetrate deeply into that culture. A sizeable place must be given to *study and research* if we are to better understand the demands and preconditions underlying the evangelization of cultures today.

Intellectual culture, based on study, research, and contemplation, is a basic prerequisites for evangelization and service to humanity. It will be the subject matter of my final chapter.

PART FOUR

CULTURE AND THE HUMAN SPIRIT

Defending culture means defending the creative freedom of the human mind and spirit, whose grandeur lies in embracing all the forms of truth and beauty. Culture, whether spontaneous or cultivated, is always straining toward the true and the beautiful. In their maturity cultures contribute the riches of knowledge, science, and artistic creation, which become the common heritage of the human family.

Today the *legitimation of science and the arts* is being posed as a problem. The scientific realm has acquired an unlimited and paradoxical power that evokes admiration, astonishment, anxiety, and even violent protest in varying degrees. Scientists cannot evade their enormous responsibility vis-à-vis the future of human societies. Modern science no longer hesitates to ponder the question of meaning, and it is becoming more open and receptive to knowledge of the absolute. Science and culture have linked destiny. Only together can they progress.

Artistic creators are also wondering about their situation in technological society and a media culture. They are well aware of being at the heart of our era's contradictions. What finer contribution could they make to the cultures of tomorrow than a contemplative attention to the enchantments of a nature that is seriously threatened today? The world needs artists to reveal humanity to itself in its sublime or tragic universe. Without beauty and admiration there would be no culture at all.

It is a sign of the time that the Church has entered into a new dialogue with modern science and art. Does that not give us reason to have hopes for the future of culture?

9/The Church and the Arts and Sciences

Defending the freedom of human intelligence and its cultural creations is an eminent form of service to modern society. The Church realizes the full importance of the issue, all the more so that it senses its natural bond with all those men and women dedicated to the quest for truth and beauty. That is why Vatican II invited Christians to undertake broad, open dialogue with scientists and artists. In this chapter we shall consider the present-day stance of the Church vis-à-vis the realms of science and the arts: activities in which human beings reveal the highest capabilities of their spirit and their consuming thirst for beauty and truth.

First, we shall consider the Church's relationship with the world of *science*. Two main topics will be examined: the relationship between faith and science, and the responsibilities of scientists in today's world. We shall see that the first topic has long occupied the Church's attention, and that a new relationship between the Church and scientists is taking center stage after a long period of serious incomprehension and mutual mistakes. With respect to the second topic, the responsibility of scientists, we find that the issue is taking on ever increasing importance in the collective conscience and in the teaching of the Church.

SCIENCE AND FAITH

A new type of dialogue is taking shape between the Church and the scientific world. This rapprochement between the scientific world and the Catholic Church is an event of immense cultural significance. Receiving a large group of Nobel Prize winners on May 9, 1983, John Paul II told them: "Your presence here has highly symbolic value in my eyes because it testifies that a fruitful dialogue is under way between the Church and science."[1]

It must be admitted that the relationship between science and Christianity has not always been an easy one, however. As *Gaudium et Spes* put it: "Although the Church has contributed much to the development of culture, experience shows that, due to circumstances, it is sometimes difficult to harmonize culture with Christianity."[2]

Further on in this chapter we shall see that the attitude and approach of the present-day Church (e.g., in the Galilei case) has helped greatly to clarify positions on both sides. But there is good reason to take note of the conflict between science and faith during the last century and to realize that the actions of the Holy See, together with the evolution of scientific culture itself, helped to place the whole question in a new perspective involving research and mutual understanding. This new outlook would find concrete form and expression at Vatican II.

The Lessening of Tensions

During the last century tension grew between the Church and modern disciplines when liberalism and positivism attacked the traditional positions of the Church in the name of new sciences and philosophies. Leo XIII courageously took up this challenge, pointing out in various ways that these calumnies grossly contradicted the real attitude of the Church toward science, research, and philosophy.

Leo XIII pointed out that the Church welcomes everything that would enlarge the domain of science, allow better exploration of nature, and contribute to the improvement of the human condition. There could be no contradiction between the truths discovered by science and divinely revealed truths because all truth derives form God.[3] This is the basic principle that Vatican II would explicitly reaffirm some eighty years later.

Leo XIII also gave impetus to the revival of a philosophy that was Christian in its inspiration, and he rebutted the unfounded accusations that such a philosophy was an obstacle to the progress of the natural sciences.[4] He also came to the defense of the ecclesiastical magisterium: "Far from being an obstacle to the love of knowledge and the advancement of the sciences, far from in any way retarding the progress of civilization, the teaching of the Church offers sure guidance and light."[5]

The tension between the teaching Church and the most quali-
fied representatives of scholarly knowledge gradually lessened,
thanks to the intellectual reforms carried out by such popes as Leo
XIII, Pius XI, Pius XII, and Paul VI. They helped to make clear the
almost connatural interest of the Church in scientific progress, the
latter being one of the major characteristics of modern culture.

Pius XI can be credited with inaugurating a thoroughgoing
reform of ecclesiastical studies. In his famous document, *Deus
Scientiarum Dominus* (1931), he insisted that departments of ecclesiastical sciences measure up to the most rigorous requirements of
university life and scientific methods, and that all candidates for
higher studies be seriously introduced to advances in the physical
and human sciences.

During his long pontificate Pius XII gave the whole world
striking testimony of the Holy See's interest in all the sciences,
welcoming countless delegations of experts and specialists in every
descipline. His imposing collection of talks and writings include
many addressed to specialists in the many modern disciplines. In
every case his words matched their interest because he knew how
to speak their language, ease their concerns, and show how
Christian morality could offer a response to their ethical problems
and deontological demands.

Paul VI was equally attentive to the realms of science, culture,
and the arts. This is obvious in his many talks and in his most
important documents. In *Populorum Progressio* (1967) he underlined
the important role of science and technology. In *Octogesima Adveniens* (1971) he offered a penetrating analysis of the role of the
human sciences.[6] Paul VI also quickly committed himself to implementing the recommendations of Vatican II concerning university
life (*Gravissimum Educationis*, nn. 10–12). He encouraged wide
consultation with universities, which led to a declaration by
Catholic universities at a 1972 convention in Rome: *The Catholic
University in the Modern World*. Even earlier, in 1968, the Congregation for Catholic Education had issued its norms (*Normae Quaedam*)
for the reform of ecclesiastical departments. After several years of
consultation and experimentation the apostolic constitution *Sa-
pienta Christiana*, dealing with ecclesiastical studies, was issued by
John Paul II in 1979.

The Holy See's dialogue with the university world is an active
and ongoing affair.

RESPECT FOR THE ORDERS OF KNOWLEDGE

We can say, then that in the modern era there has been a profound change in relationships between the scientific world and the Church. Vatican II bears clear witness to this fact. *Gaudium et Spes* teaches that earthly realities have their own proper laws and values, hence their "demand for autonomy is entirely legitimate." This autonomy is in line with the will of the Creator, who endowed all things with "their own stability, truth, goodness, proper laws, and order." We must respect these things and "the appropriate methods of the individual sciences and arts."

We should not harbor any trace of fear, as if scientific research could threaten faith or morality: "If methodological investigation in each branch of learning is carried out in a genuinely scientific manner and in accord with moral norms, it never really conflicts with faith. For earthly matters and the concerns of faith derive from the same God." Indeed, the honest researcher may be led invisibly by the God of truth.

Gaudium et Spes goes further and deplores the unjustified fear of science displayed by some Catholics: "We cannot but deplore certain habits of mind, sometimes found among Christians too, which do not pay sufficient attention to the rightful independence of science." But the autonomy of science vis-à-vis religion certainly cannot be equated with rejection of God, for the creature has no meaning without its Creator: "When God is forgotten, the creature becomes unintelligible."[7]

Exploring the issue further, *Gaudium et Spes* acknowledged that more recent lines of research might well pose new problems to faith itself. That only means that theologians will have to undertake original research of their own: "Theologians are invited to seek continually for more suitable ways to communicate doctrine to the human beings of their day." Pastors, too, must take into account the new scientific culture and be willing to use the modern disciplines in their work: "In pastoral care there must be adequate familiarity with, not only theological principles, but also the findings of the secular sciences, of psychology and sociology in particular."[8]

The present attitude of the Church toward science is clearly illustrated by its current stance on the Galileo case, which for centuries had been cited as proof of Catholic intolerance of science.

THE GALILEO CASE AND FREEDOM OF INQUIRY

Speaking to the Pontifical Academy of Sciences in 1979, John Paul II asked that the historical debate over Galileo Galilei be reopened with complete frankness and objectivity. Theologians, scientists, and historians were asked to reexamine the Galileo case "with honest admission of mistakes on whichever side they may have occurred."[9]

John Paul II again brought up the Galileo case when he spoke to winners of the Nobel Prize in 1983.[10] He reminded them that it led to serious misunderstandings between the Church and the scientific world. Only patient, humble reexamination on both sides helped to dispel those misunderstandings and thereby benefit both parties: "The Church and science itself have benefited greatly by discovering, through reflection and sometimes painful experiences, the pathways to truth and objective knowledge." For its part the Church, through a process of maturation and intellectual purification, came to better appreciate the difference between scientific theory and divine revelation. The Bible does not contain any physical or astronomical theory, and "the Holy Spirit does not in any way guarantee any explanations we might like to uphold about the physical makeup of reality." Like any other historical institution, the Church was part and parcel of a cultural era and its conditionings. This experience "led Catholics to a more correct understanding of their own faith and its proper domain." Science and faith represent two different orders of knowledge that are autonomous in their processes; in the last analysis, they both contribute to the discovery of the whole truth, which has its origin in God.

Scientists and scholars, for their part, have also proceeded to a critique of their own methods and objectives: "Is it not obvious today that the greater sensitivity of scientists and researchers to the values of the spirit and morality are adding a new dimension to your disciplines and opening them bravely to the universal?" The Church appeals to the investigative capabilities of scientists and pleads that "no limit be set on our common quest for knowledge." Science cannot close itself to the universal and the absolute, nor to knowledge of wholes: "Allow the inclinations of your spirit to lead you to the universal and the absolute. More than ever, our world needs minds capable of embracing wholes and advancing cognition toward humanized knowledge and wisdom."[11]

The Church's dialogue with scientists and scholars is not simply apologetic or defensive in nature. It positively seeks to promote the preconditions for scientific and intellectual creativity. In this dialogue the Church situates itself clearly on the cultural plane and joins scientists in reflecting on the *meaning* of science. Speaking to Spanish university personnel John Paul II reminded them of the "perduring preconditions for intellectual creativity." Four main points were stressed: freedom of inquiry, joint study, openness to the universal, and knowledge conceived as service to the whole human being. The Church, he said, is on the side of research and its freedom because it is a quest for truth: "The Church upholds freedom of inquiry, which is one of the noblest attributes of the human being. It is through inquiry and research that humanity arrives at Truth, which is one of the most beautiful names for God."[12] Our age needs a science of *homo*, and original research is in order: "Alongside the physical and biological sciences, specialists in the human sciences must be enlisted . . . in the service of the human being and the defence of its identity, dignity, and moral grandeur. In the Church's viewpoint, science and culture cannot possibly be dissociated."[13]

Speaking in Cologne to men and women of science and culture (Nov. 15, 1980), John Paul II acknowledged the crucial role of the *human sciences* in the transformation of modern societies: "The human and social sciences, as well as the cultural sciences, philosophy, and theology, have in many ways stimulated the modern human being's reflection on itself and its existence in a world dominated by science and technical expertise."

To be concrete, we can say that the human sciences have made possible *the social system of modern states*: their educational and cultural activities, their government administration, their economic processes, and their health provisions. These sciences have served the socio-cultural progress of humanity. Faith has not been alone in perceiving the dignity of the human being. Natural reason, too, "is capable of this insight," and it has helped greatly to explore in depth the notion of human rights. Thanks to a new methodological approach, the conflicts between faith and reason have been able to be resolved: "We can now say that such conflicts are a thing of the past, thanks to the persuasive force of science and, above all, to the labors of a scientific theology that has deepened our understanding of the faith and liberated it from time-bound conditioning factors."[14]

THE CRISIS OF SCIENTIFIC CULTURE

But these sciences can go astray if they cease to pursue their ultimate aim: namely, service to culture, hence to humanity. They are then in danger of being corrupted, of becoming technological instrument of domination of manipulation in the service of economic or political ends.[15] The *legitimation of science* is now *in crisis*. Science faces this sort of crisis when it is reduced to a merely functionalist or utilitarian model. When science is dissociated from truth and service to the human being, it is in danger of turning against human beings. That explains the virulence of antiscientific and anti-intellectual currents, which have their own hidden risks: that is, irrationalism, nihilism, and instinct-driven behavior. It also points up the urgent need to uphold an authentic science, a science open to exploring *the meaning of the human being* and seeking *the whole truth*.

The Church does not hesitate to become the advocate of science, in the name of the human being's freedom to know. It reminds us that the scientist faces basic questions: for example, What is the role and purpose of science? We must remember that science, in and of itself, "is not in a position to answer the question of meaning." Our scientific and technological culture is in crisis because it has forgotten the whole human being and disregarded the first and foremost value: that is, the quest for truth.

While fully respecting the methodological exigencies of abstraction and specialized analysis, science must never diregard the "unitary direction" of knowledge: "There is no reason for not taking a position in favor of truth or for being afraid of the truth." The reason is that science, too, is a way to truth. That is what scientists discover on their pathway as they hone their intelligence, for that intelligence comes from God and is destined for truth, not error. Only in this way can they overcome the *crisis of legitimation* facing science: "A science that is free and dependent solely on truth will not allow itself to be reduced to a functionalist model or anything else of that sort that limits the cognitive field of scientific rationality."

Note the paradoxical turn of events. The Church, once accused of obscurantism, has now made itself the advocate of science, reason, and freedom of inquiry: "In the past, some precursors of modern science combatted the Church in the name of reason, liberty, and progress. Today, with the crisis of meaning facing science, the many threats to its freedom, and the problematic character of progress, the battlefronts are reversed."[16] Now we find the Church defending the cause and legitimacy of authentic science.

CHURCH AND SCIENCE: A CONNATURAL TIE

There is a basic reason why the Church defends modern science, despite certain antagonism of the past. There is a connatural tie between science and the Church. The tie is even more obvious in the case of science and research carried out in a university setting. In a message to university researchers and professors in Central America, John Paul II noted that the university and the Church, each in its own way, are dedicated to the search for truth, the progress of the human mind and spirit, universal values, exploration of the mysteries of the universe, and understanding of the human being, and the complete development of the human being. He expressed similar thoughts in Manila in 1981, pointing out that the words "catholicity" and "university" are practically synonymous. Neither the Church nor the university admits of frontiers.[17]

John Paul II was explicit and insistent in his address to university personnel in Central America, where human dignity is especially threatened:

> The Church addresses itself in a special way to today's university people to tell them that we must work together to defend the human being, whose dignity and honor are seriously threatened. By vocation the university is a disinterested and free institution. Together with the Church, it is one of the few institutions in modern society that is capable of defending the human being for its own sake, without subterfuge of pretext, for the simple reason that human beings have a unique dignity and deserve to be respected for themselves.[18]

If we are to render authentic service to humanity, then science and ethics cry out for each other. Research does indeed require special aptitude and intelligence, but it also requires a moral attitude that John Paul II chose to stress in his Hiroshima talk of 1981. He acknowledged the professional and ethical merits of many scientists who may not even profess any religion. He noted that the Church appreciates their intellectual honesty, their quest for truth, their self-discipline, their objectivity, their commitment to serve humanity, and their respect for the the mysteries of the universe. They form "a great spiritual family" with all those who have faith in the human being's spiritual vocation. And so it is that science links up with the highest exigencies of culture: "In a word, the human being must be loved for itself. This in the supreme value that all sincere humanists, all magnanimous thinkers, and all the great religion seek to promote."[19]

Returning to the same issue in an address to the Pontifical Academy of Sciences, John Paul II summed up his own thinking by mentioning four basic values that must be safeguarded in the practice of science: "Truth, freedom, justice, and love: these are the fundamental axes of the generous choice you have made for a science that builds peace. Those four values, axes of science and of civilized societal life, should undergird the universal appeal of scientists, the cultural world, and the world's citizens."[20] The Church's appeal to scientists is basically aimed at redefining their mission in society in terms of responsible service.

THE RESPONSIBILITY OF SCIENTISTS

THEIR CONSIDERABLE MORAL AUTHORITY

Today science does not just pose epistemological problems. Even more importantly, perhaps, it poses questions of collective ethics because science now wields enormous resposibility in society. It has even become an *institution* in modern countries, a seat of power and authority. The "scientific sector" or the "scientific community" is capable of admirable achievements and lethal productions. Given this context, scientists have a new responsibility. The future of our societies and of all humanity depends on their moral attitude, as John Paul II pointed out to Spanish university personnel: "You men and women who represent science and culture have considerable moral authority. Thanks to your prestige, you jointly can see to it that the scientific sector serves human culture first, and that it is never used to destroy that culture."[21]

In his address to UNESCO, John Paul II expressed his deep concern over this matter. The future of the human race, he said, cannot be dissociated from the future of science and culture. He would not be fulfilling the duties of his office if he did not speak out on this serious issue. Defending science and culture comes down to defending the destiny of humanity and the world. Despite the undoubtedly high-minded intentions of scientists, humanity and the world are threatened at their very core. We must

know how to look reality in the face. If science overlooks conscience, it is in danger of pursuing destructive and lethal ends, "to
a degree never known before, causing truly unimaginable sorts of
damage." For today science and technology help to prepare arms
that can be catastrophic for the future of the human race.

John Paul II pleads vigorously for a moral advance on the part of
scientists. Indeed, it is a moral imperative: "We must mobilize
consciences . . . increase the efforts of human consciences." The
primacy of ethics is here the golden rule that is ultimately required
by "the human being's transcendence over the world and God's
transcendence over the human being." The Church appeals to the
considerable moral power and authority vested in today's scientific
community: "All together, you are an enormous force, the force of
minds and consciences. . . . Men and women of science, commit
all your moral authority to saving humanity from nuclear
destruction."[22] John Paul II reiterated the same principle in 1983,
when he addressed the Pontifical Academy of Sciences. And he
assured its members that the Church is their ally in this fight on
behalf of humanity: "The Catholic Church is your ally, this Church
that loves true science and right thinking."[23]

ROLE OF THE WORLD SCIENTIFIC COMMUNITY

A very promising cultural and ethical development in today's
world is the emergence of a *worldwide scientific community* aware of
its moral authority and its responsibilities. John Paul II has
addressed himself on several occasions to the scientific community
and asked it to commit itself to working for peace, development,
and human liberation. Its power of cultural creation is enormous,
he points out, and he has only admiration for the fact that the
collaboration of scientists around the world has resulted in discoveries greatly benefiting humanity and its advancement. In the
same 1983 address to the Pontifical Academy of Sciences mentioned above, John Paul II cited several examples of such collaboration: the fight against epidemics and diseases, the discovery of
new food resources, the intensification of communications, and
defense against natural catastrophes.[24] But scientists must remain
on the alert, lest their power be exploited against the welfare of
humanity.

With a boldness that caught the attention of the world press,
John Paul II called upon the world's scientists to oppose the use of
science for purposes of aggression and military destruction. Scien-

tists should not abdicate their liberty. They must preserve their right to choose their area of research. If they foresee that their research, in very concrete circumstances, will be used for lethal ends, they should make their opposition felt so that "the laboratories and factories of death may give way to laboratories of life."

The world's scientists should be united in this no to death, thereby disarming science and transforming it into an instrument of peace instead. Scientists must exercise their full freedom: "When, in a given historical situation, it is almost inevitable that some form of scientific research will be used for aggressive purposes, scientists should make a choice that will enable them to work together for the welfare of human beings, for the construction of peace. In rejecting certain areas of research because they inevitably will be destined for lethal ends in concrete historical circumstances, the world's scientists should be united by a common will to disarm science and to constitute a providential force for peace."

John Paul II compares scientists to medical doctors, who take an oath to use their skills to cure diseases. This calls for a liberation of their human mind and intelligence, and it must be translated into action whenever some party wants "to do violence to you," to "exploit your research and discoveries against justice and peace."[25]

Furthermore, the international scientific community cannot be subjected to the domination of a few powers or nations. It must be free and open to all nations and research centers. Says John Paul II: "It is not enough that political colonialism has disappeared. All forms of scientific and technological colonialism must also end." The Church is delighted that it can dialogue with scientists of every nation, regardless of race or religion: "This is a form of cultural ecumenism that the Church, promoter of a real religious ecumenism, cannot help but view with profound satisfaction." Scientists all over the world have the duty of making sure that "scientific discoveries are not put in the service of war, tyranny, or terror. The firm determination to orient science toward the promotion of justice and peace calls for great love for humanity."[26]

These words bring us back to another problem of basic importance today: the role of science and technology in the pursuit of development and peace. It is an issue I considered in chapter 4 when I dealt with the links between culture, justice, and peace.

And so I come to the second major topic in this chapter: the relationship between the Church and the arts.

THE CHURCH AND THE ARTS

To deal adequately with this vast topic we would have to traverse practically the whole history of the Church. As Vatican II pointed out, the Church has always promoted the liberal arts, trained artists, and inspired works and monuments that have immeasurably enriched the human heritage.[27] Sticking to the framework of this volume, however, I shall consider *the more recent teaching* of the Church regarding its relationship with the world of culture and the arts.

Pius XII was particularly attentive to artists, their productions, and their responsibilities in the contemporary world; he often welcomed them in special audiences. But it was mainly with Vatican II and Paul VI that the Church's discourse on the issue of art became more incisive and moved toward a very frank and promising dialogue.

Difficult Relationships

Vatican II reminds us that the Church has always promoted the arts, and that it has encouraged and even trained artists over the centuries. Even granting that, however, we must admit that in the modern age the relationship between artists and the Catholic world grew considerably cooler. This situation was well analyzed in a talk that Paul VI gave to artists assembled in the Sistine Chapel in May 1964. He noted that artists have always had a relationship with the popes. But these relationships have changed: "One might even go so far as to say that the thread of this relationship has been lost."[28]

One theme stressed by Paul VI is that the Church always needs artists. This is not solely because it must order works designed for cultic worship. "Nor is it solely because a tradition of sumptuousness, patronage, grandeur, and pageantry surrounds its ministry, its authority, and its relations with human beings, or because it needs this decorative and expressive framework." Paul VI offers a deeper and more intrinsic reason. The ministry of the Church is to preach and reveal the realm of the spirit, the realm of the ineffable and of God. And, says Paul VI to artists: "In this operation, which translates the invisible world into accessible, intelligible forms, it is you who are the masters." If the Church were deprived of their cooperation, its ministry would suffer: "It would have to try to become artistic and even prophetic. . . . It would have to make the priesthood coincide with art." And what about artists? Are they not discovering that the homeland of the ineffable "is still faith, prayer, religion"?

Both parties must recognize that friendship should be reestablished: "Our relationships are a bit impaired. We have not broken off our friendship but we have muddied it." With complete frankness Paul VI listed the complaints that might be voiced by one or the other side. Some of today's artistic creations grieve the Church, which considers itself "the guardian of humanity" and its highest culture: "These artistic expressions offend us, we who are the guardians of all humanity, of the complete definition of the human being, of its moral healthiness and its stability." Going further, Paul VI alludes to certain art forms detached from life, whose expression is confused: "One does not know what you are saying. Quite often, you yourselves do not know. . . . We are left surprised, intimidated, distant." At the same time, however, the Church admires the long patience and searching involved in artistic creation, which requires "an apprenticeship that is hard, long, ascetic, slow, and gradual."

But the Church is also ready to admit its own faults, says Paul VI. In the past it imposed on artists a rule or norm that was too rigid and passive: the rule of imitation. "We have sometimes imposed on you a leaden cope. One could well put it that way. Please forgive us for that." Paul VI admits that artists have been misunderstood, even offended: "We did not explain ourselves to you. . . . That is why you did not come to know us. . . . We shall carry our *mea culpa* through to the end. We have trespassed against you by resorting to counterfeits, oleography, and cheap art." Paul VI makes this confession even though it must be recognized that the Church has not always had the resources to pay for great new works worthy of admiration.

A NEW ACCORD?

But why should not a new accord between the Church and artists be possible today? Vatican II had already proposed a great pact for a new alliance with artists. Alluding to the Constitution on the Sacred Liturgy that had just been promulgated by Vatican II, Paul VI said: "Our pact is signed. It only awaits your signature in turn." The doors of the Church are open to welcome artists, said

Paul VI: "Come and draw from us the motif, theme, and sometimes even more than that for your work: the secret fluid known as
inspiration, grace, the charism of art."

In 1973, with 270 artists in attendance, Paul VI inaugurated a
new collection of religious art for the Vatican museums. The
ceremony took place in the Sistine Chapel, "one of the most
evocative and stimulating wonders of human civilization." Paul VI
wondered if our age is still capable of producing religious art: "Is
religious art the product of an earlier stage of the human spirit that
is now past?" The Church had taught, cultivated, and preserved
the arts. But does it have anything to offer today besides museums
of ancient art? Has its great tradition grown sterile?[29]

Paul VI tried to get across the point that the Church is always
open to art even in its most daring and modern forms. He sought
to understand the inner psychology of the present-day artist, to
discover "that art which is born more from within than without,"
to read "the soul of the artist and even the modern soul . . . the
soul of the spontaneously religious human being." The modern
artist is more subjective, and many creators "have replaced esthetics with psychology."

In a manner very typical of Paul VI, he asked whether modern
art was sill balanced and worthy of the human being. He replied:
"It seems to us that it is not true to say that the criteria governing
contemporary art bear only the marks of madness, passion, purely
cerebral and arbitrary abstraction." He reiterated his hope in the
gifts of modern artists: "In their own way they are the prophets
and poets of today's human being, of human mentality, of modern
society." Our modern society is secularized and tainted by "ob-
scenities and blasphemies." But again and again we find that
amazing capacity "to express not only what is authentically human
but also what is religious, divine, and Christian."

THE CHURCH'S NEED FOR ARTISTS

John Paul II has taken bold action to make clear the high
significance of art for the Church. He did not hesitate to visit the
opera at La Scala in Milan: "A pope at La Scala in Milan is an
extraordinary event that is hard to define. . . . But for me it is an
act of being present in the world of art." The artistic world is
bound up with countless personalities who, even today, "make up
a large part of world civilization." The Church wants to be close to
the truth of art and the truth of life. That is why it respects "the

sense and soundness of culture and art, welcoming truth wherever it is found." We must defend the freedom of art and oppose all efforts to dominate or manipulate culture: "It is not permissible to try to sequester culture in a single direction, turning one's nose up at faith, or replacing it with nondescript substitutes."

The Church needs artists, and John Paul II calls them his friends: "Be present with your art, with the prestige and magisterium of our art." Together the Church and artists must practice "an ecology of the spirit in the service of human beings . . . whom the great Ambrose of Milan called 'the most beautiful work in the world . . . the synthesis of the universe and the supreme beauty among the world's creatures.'" Every great artistic creation is a spiritual revelation: "Every great work of art . . . is religious in its inspiration and its roots."[30]

A visit to Venice enabled John Paul II to celebrate its amazing expressions of architecture, music, and painting. The city of Venice itself has become art, "hence light, color, line, space, harmony . . . an architecture embellishing space that has been rendered luminous by sea and sky." Venice is the "city of humanity," the "city of civilization," and its genial artists have left their mark on the culture of Europe's great centers. The exemplary experience of Venice teaches us that art is a language of universality and transcendence, "an original language that probes beyond immediate experience to the primary and ultimate meaning of life." Thus, art has a religious dimension: "Because it prompts human beings to take cognizance of the restlessness at the core of their being, a restlessness that can never be satisfied by science or technology." The artist has an irreplaceable vocation in society: "Art is a 'grace' given to some to allow them to open the way for others. . . . It reveals transcendence. . . . Without art the world would lose its most beautiful course."[31]

Another idea dear to John Paul II is that art can become a means of communion and reconciliation in a world torn by divisions. On the occasion of a symposium dealing with the Russian poet, Vyaceslav Ivanov (1866–1949), the pope expressed the hope "we might be able to restore the lost unity of East and West, of North and South, breathing deeply and peacefully at the heart of the ecumene." He reminded the cultural representatives present at the symposium of their role in effecting reconciliation: "Your cultural action, combined with that of poets, thinkers, and artists, is at the very heart of this vital rapprochement."[32] The pope cites Ivanov himself to prove that every culture has its deepest roots in a religious core: "For every great culture, insofar as it issues from memory, is the incarnation of a fundamental spiritual reality; it can only be the multiple expression of a religious idea that constitutes its core."

Speaking familiarly to students in Gniezno in 1979, John Paul II reminded them that he himself has been shaped by the artistic and literary tradition of their common homeland: "The man speaking to you owes his own spiritual formation, from the very beginning, to Polish culture: to Poland's literature, music, plastic arts, and theater; to Polish history and its Christian traditions; to Polish schools and universities." This artistic tradition finds its source and roots in the Christian faith: "The inspiration of Christianity ever remains the principal source of the creativity of Polish artists."[33]

In 1983 John Paul II bestowed the title of "blessed" on Fra Angelico.[34] In February 1984 he proclaimed him the patron of artists. The pope noted "the exceptional, mystical fascination" of Fra Angelico's painting, whose whole life bore witness to the vital bond that can be established between faith and art: "In his own life he verified the essential, organic link existing between Christianity and culture, between the human being and culture. In him faith became culture, and culture became faith actually lived." He exemplified a twofold creativity: "He created his works of art and, at the same time, he created himself." Holy Scripture had been his main source of inspiration; that is why we find a "gospel sense of proportion" in him. John Paul II invites all artists to seek the same integration and perfection: "Strive for a suitable proportion between the beauty of your works and the beauty of your soul."[35]

Speaking to artists in Vienna in 1983, John Paul II addressed the same theme. Human beings need art. The Church, too, needs artists, for reasons that go beyond the mere need for art works: "To gain a wider and deeper experience of the human condition, of humanity's glories and miseries. The Church needs the arts to come to know better the deeper depths of the human being, to whom it is supposed to preach the gospel message."

But, notes the pope, the modern conscience is faced with further questions. Is art still possible? Do not the death of God and the death of the human being mark the death of art itself and its humanist pretensions? Some even feel that the arts face the same fate as philosophy and the Church itself: "We often hear talk of the decline of the arts as an imminent or already accomplished fact.

The arts, the philosophy as well, will share the same fate as the Church."

John Paul II rejects this pessimism: "Because I am convinced of the inexhaustible potential of the human spirit and of the power of the human imagination." He is delighted that dialogue is slowly beginning again between the arts and the Church. This encouraging fact may lead in the future "to works of art that will again open the eyes and ears and hearts of persons who believe and who are searching."[36] Here we have the most solid support for the legitimation of art, and it is revealing that the Church has become its advocate for reasons that go to the very core of human cultures.

THE WORLD'S NEED FOR BEAUTY

The teachings of the present pope and his immediate predecessors reflect and extend the guidelines set forth by Vatican II. That council affirmed the cultural significance of art, urging Christians to understand artists and the newer forms of creative expression. *Gaudium et Spes* defended freedom of inquiry and research in the scientific realm and in the realm of artistic creation. Even if certain agnostic strains often leave their mark on literary creations and contemporary esthetics, that should not prevent us from recognizing the lofty civilizing capabilities of intellectual and artistic creations. When human beings devote themselves creatively to the arts, sciences, and culture:

> [They] can do very much to elevate the human family to a more sublime understanding of truth, goodness, and beauty, and to the formation of judgments which embody universal values. Thus humanity can be more clearly enlightened by that marvelous wisdom that was with God from all eternity.[37]

Another conciliar document, *Inter Mirifica* brought out the role of art in revealing the human being when it asked if art could *represent evil*. The answer was yes, but certain conditions had to be met. On the one hand: "With the help of the media of social communication too, the narration, description, or portrayal of moral evil can indeed serve to make the human being more deeply known and studied, and to reveal and enhance the grandeur of truth and goodness. Such aims are achieved by means of appropriately heightened dramatic effects." On the other hand: "Moral norms must prevail if spiritual profit rather than harm is to ensue.

This requirement is especially needed when the subjects treated are entitled to reverence, or may all too easily trigger base desires in human beings."[38]

At the end of Vatican II, the council fathers addressed one special appeal to artists in general: poets and literary masters, painters, sculptors, architects, musicians, those devoted to the theater and the cinema. Their age-old alliance with the Church is noted, and the hope is expressed that it will continue: "Do not allow an alliance as fruitful as this to be broken. . . . This world in which we live needs beauty in order not to sink into despair. . . . Remember that you are the guardians of beauty in the world."

Vatican II did not hesitate to rank art among the loftiest activities of the human spirit, especially when artistic creation seeks to express the mystery and splendor of the divine:

> The fine arts are very rightly considered to rank among the noblest expressions of the human spirit. This judgment applies especially to religious art and to its highest achievement, sacred art. By their very nature they seek to express in some way, in human works, the infinite beauty of God. To the extent that they aim exclusively at turning human hearts to God . . . they are dedicated to the greater honor and glory of God.[39]

The *religious character of art* is a theme highlighted by John Paul II on more than one occasion. Of course the Church rightly honors artists who draw their inspiration from sacred history and the liturgy. The Bible, in particular, "has never ceased to be a source of inspiration for artists of all sorts: architects, sculptors, painters, poets, composers of musical works and hymns, authors of plays, movies, and choreography." But art in and of itself, in its creative tension, already entails a religious dimension: "Its course is a little like that of faith itself. . . . The essential element of art lies in the innermost depths of the human being, where the yearning to give meaning to one's life is accompanied by a fleeting intuition of the beauty and mysterious unity of things."

Art is also a symbolic expression of love, for it is communication between human beings: "Yes, art is a privileged expression of the sympathy extended to one human being by another, of the love for what is deepest in the human being. . . . A world without art is in danger of being a world closed to love." In an age like ours, when a veil of sadness covers our culture, art is a summons to hope: "Our world needs beauty so as not to sink into despair."[40]

Of all the arts, music manages to exalt the universal harmony by overcoming all barriers and directly addressing the human heart: "It is an expression of freedom that escapes all authority. It offers a haven of utmost independence." It creates "a common homeland" for all musicians. It sets the harmonies of the heart resonating and awakens deep emotions. Its ability to penetrate hearts can create a fraternity of human spirits and lead human beings to the loftiest heights. Linked to cultic worship, music becomes the suggestive and solemn support of prayer and our glorification of God.[41]

So there is a connaturality and spiritual partnership between the arts and religion. The pathways of art and the pathways of the Church meet where the human spirit throbs in its search for identity and the absolute.

Art is one of the noblest expressions of human culture. The great writers, genial creators, poets, and artists reveal the human being to itself, its tragic fragility and its yearning for immortality. That is why masterpieces belong to world culture and the whole human family.

The Church is keenly aware that it is serving culture when it reminds our contemporaries of the indispensable role played by intellectual and artistic creation. For such creation bears witness to the human vocation to freedom of spirit and transcendence. In becoming the advocate of art, knowledge, and research, the Church is ultimately defending an image of the human being as a creator of culture and a being capable of self-transcendence. This is a sign of hope for the cultures now emerging in the world.

Afterword: Toward New Cultures

At the end of this analysis I feel one compelling conclusion: the urgent need to *pose* the problem of cultures *in a new way*. If we realize and appreciate the fact that culture is essentially the product of our living experience, we will succeed in mastering our future. And we shall do that by ceaselessly re-creating our own culture, that image of ourselves that is ever the same and ever being reborn, ever fragile and ever perfectible. There we have a *prospective view of culture*, one which compels us to move beyond the mere conditionings of our history and ethically shoulder our collective future, believing all the while that this is possible.

In the light of what has been said in these pages, I am invited to prolong my reflection by posing some questions under five basic heads.

1. If the human being truly is a *creator of culture*, must we not leave a lot of room for confidence? The cultures of the future are already gestating, and they will prove to be what our own choices have imagined and willed for our collective destiny. As I see it, culture cannot possibly be a mere reflex or conditioning process, although this is the false idea of culture circulating in some milieus afflicted with an unwitting fatalism that has been spawned by increasingly depersonalized societies subject to the constraints of ideologies or selfish interests. I believe that a cultural mobilization can again give human form to even the most complex societies. It is a radical question: How can we together remain responsible masters of the cultures that are emerging? I choose to look beyond cultural determinism, confident that we can freely shoulder our human culture.

2. We also ask: How do today's men and women plan to promote a cultural project for tomorrow that will be based on the values of fellowship, justice, solidarity, and dignity for all? For every culture, *the ideal future is in the nature of a promise and a*

mobilizing prospect. Will creative forms of expertise and artistic genius have their rightful place in the cultures now taking shape? Will they be open to the mystery of the human being and the grandeur of its destiny? The crisis of the present-day world gives us a firm conviction that is in the nature of a hope: the future of the human being will depend on our enlightened choices, our collective courage, and the new cultures we shall create together. Conscience and culture will henceforth be linked in solidarity.

3. The fight for justice is characteristic of our age. But does it always pursue the defense of culture with the same determination? Political decision-makers and militants must realize that *culture is just as primary a need* as biological needs are. There cannot be any acceptable justice without the defense of the cultural values that give collectivities a reason for living with dignity. And, on the other side of the coin, there is no true culture without justice for each and all. Thus development, justice, peace, and culture can only grow together. How can we get across this primary datum of anthropology to present-day public opinion and the politicians of tomorrow?

4. Today socio-political projects give more room to cultural objectives. Almost all governments are pursuing a "cultural policy." This must be considered real progress in the practice of politics insofar as it places human aims above narrowly economic goals. But it also raises new questions. How exactly are we to understand *the role of government vis-à-vis culture*? If government must make an effort to equalize the opportunities of all citizens and groups to enjoy and create cultural goods, what process of self-control will keep it from confusing or equating cultural action and political calculation? Enlightened public opinion also faces certain questions: for example, What form of civic vigilance will enable it to simultaneously encourage and criticize government policies in the vast domain of culture, which includes basic education, continuing education, communication, and scientific research? Socio-political democracy calls for cultural democracy as well. And, it must be added, political liberation goes by way of cultural liberation.

5. The rise of new cultures represents a great hope and a great challenge for Christians. They must first envision the future in an enlarged perspective and convince themselves that *the realm of culture is to be the preferred field of priority action for them.* Have they adequately learned to perceive the hopes and expectations of their milieu? How can they facilitate their own culture's encounter with

the gospel message? What concrete meaning will they give to "the evangelization of cultures"? Since Vatican II, the whole Church has been committed to redefining its approach to the contemporary world. Hence inculturation is a concern of all local Churches in every part of the world. So there is an urgent need for reflection, research, and concerted action involving all Christians in collaboration with all persons of good will to seek the humanization of cultures.

And what about those cultures of the future? If our future does indeed depend on culture, it ultimately comes down to one question: "What sort of culture will we be wise enough to build together? In the core and heart of today's socio-cultures, there must be a common commitment of conscience to defend the human being and its culture. And Christians should be the first to believe that the "civilization of love" will be the mobilizing project par excellence.

Notes

Chapter 1

1. Cf. Edward Tylor, *Primitive Culture* (London: John Murray, 1871), I, 1.

2. See Victor Hell, *L'Idée de culture* (Paris: Presses Universitaires de France, 1981), chap. 2, p. 24.

3. Ibid., pp. 17–30.

4. Raymond Williams, *Culture and Society: 1780–1950* (London and New York: Harper Torchbooks, 1963), p. 16. Cited in Victor Hell, *L'Idée de culture*, p. 18.

5. In *The German Ideology* Marx wrote: "The thoughts of the ruling class are also, in every age, the ruling thoughts, i.e., the class that is the ruling *material* force of society is also the ruling *spiritual* force. The class that has the means of material production at its disposal has control, at the same time, of the means of intellectual production; with the result that the thoughts of those who are denied the means of intellectual production are likewise subjected to this ruling class." See Karl Marx, *L'Idéologie allemande*, French edition presented and annotated by Gilbert Badia (Paris: Éditions sociales, 1968, p. 75).

6. Vatican II, Pastoral Constitution on the Church in Today's World, *Gaudium et Spes*, n. 53.

7. Paul VI, address at the closing of Vatican II, *Documentation Catholique* (henceforth DC), n. 1462 (1966), cols. 59–66.

8. John XXIII, address at the opening of Vatican II, October 11, 1962: DC, n. 1387 (1962), cols. 1377–86.

9. Paul VI, encyclical *Ecclesiam Suam*, August 6, 1964, nn. 66–67: DC, n. 1431 (1964), cols. 1058–93.

10. Ibid., n. 101.

11. *Gaudium et Spes*, n. 62.

12. Ibid., n. 58.

13. Ibid.

14. Vatican II, Decree on the Missionary Activity of the Church, *Ad Gentes*, n. 9.

15. Vatican II, Decree on the Apostolate of the Laity, *Apostolicam Actuositatem*, n. 7.

16. Vatican II, *Ad Gentes*, n. 11.

17. Ibid., n. 15.

18. *Epistola ad Diognetum*, n. 5: P.G., 2, 1173.

19. Vatican II, *Ad Gentes*, n. 34.

20. Vatican II, Declaration on the Relationship of the Church to Non-Christian Religions, *Nostra Aetate*, n. 2.

21. For a more detailed study of Vatican II as a cultural happening and a teaching source on the relationship between the Church and cultures, see H. Carrier, "The Contribution of the Council to Culture", in René Latourelle, ed., *Vatican II: Assessment and Perspectives*. Twenty-five Years After (1962–1987). Mahwah, N. J., Paulist Press, 1989, ch. 58; Joseph Gremillion, ed., *The Church & Culture since Vatican II*, The Experience of North and Latin America, University of Notre Dame Press, 1985.

Chapter 2

1. *Gaudium et Spes*, n. 62.
2. Leo XIII, encyclical *Inscrutabili*, April 21, 1878.
3. Leo XIII, encyclical *Immortale Dei*, Nov. 1, 1885, n. 9.
4. Ibid.
5. St. Augustine, *Epistolae*, n. 138, 5; *Ad Marcellinum*, chap. 2, 15. Cited in *Immortale Dei*, n. 8.
6. Benedict XV, encyclical *Ad Beatissimi Apostolorum*, Nov. 1, 1914, n. 20.
7. Tertullian, *Apologeticum*, n. 42.
8. Pius XI, encyclical *Quadragesimo Anno*, May 15, 1931, n. 140. See Leo XIII, encyclical *Rerum Novarum*, May 15, 1891, n. 22.
9. Pius XI, encyclical *Divini Redemptoris*, March 19, 1937, n. 1.
10. Ibid., n. 2.
11. See ibid., nn. 2, 7.
12. Pius XII, radio message, Sept. 1, 1944.
13. Pius XII, radio message, Christmas 1944, n. 19.
14. John XXIII, encyclical *Mater et Magistra*, May 15, 1961, n. 239: DC, n. 1352 (1961), cols. 945–90.
15. John XXIII, encyclical *Pacem in Terris*, April 11, 1963, n. 158: DC, n. 1398 (1963).
16. *Pacem in Terris*, n. 159.
17. François Perroux in *La Croix*, April 19, 1967.
18. *L'Osservatore Romano*, Jan. 1, 1976. See *Paul VI et la Modernité dans l'Eglise*, colloquium of the Ecole Française in Rome, June 2–4, 1983 (Rome: Ecole Française de Rome, 1984). In that volume see esp. Paul Poupard, "L'enseignement social de Paul VI," pp. 429–43.
19. John Paul II, address to Cardinals, Nov. 5, 1979: DC, n. 1775 (1979), p. 1006.
20. The cultural activity of the Holy See is considerable at various levels. Several Roman Congregations are involved in cultural issues when they deal with matters relating to doctrine, evangelization, catechesis, missions, education, liturgy, and sacred art. In the spirit of Vatican II, more recent organisms have been created to deal with ecumenism, Non-Christian religions, nonbelievers, justice and peace, the laity, the family, migrants, tourism, charitable activity and development, and the media of social communication. All of these organisms must stay in constant touch with the Church's dialogue with cultures. Furthermore, the Holy See runs universities, faculties, academies, commissions of experts, an astronomical observatory, the library and archives of the Vatican, and museums; their cultural splendor is appreciated worldwide. The Holy See is also on call to UNESCO, the Council of Europe, and the Organization of American States for any and every question dealing with humanity and culture; and each year it participates in a large number of scientific and cultural congresses.
21. Autograph letter of John Paul II to Cardinal Agostino Casaroli, Secretary of State, on the founding of the Pontifical Council for Culture, May 20, 1982: DC, n. 1832 (1982), pp. 604–6; in AAS, 74 (1983), 683–88.
22. Address to the Pontifical Council for Culture, Jan. 18, 1983: DC, n. 1845 (1983), pp. 146–48. The PCC publishes a bulletin in English, French, Italian and Spanish: "Church and Cultures."

Chapter 3

1. John Paul II, opening address at the Puebla Conference, I, 9: DC (*Documentation Catholique*), n. 1758 (1979), pp. 164–72; see p. 168.
2. John Paul II, encyclical *Redemptor Hominis*, n. 15: DC, n. 1759 (1979), p. 310.

3. Ibid., n. 17.

4. John Paul II, address to UNESCO, June 2, 1980, n. 13: DC, n. 1788 (1980), pp. 603–9. See *Redemptor Hominis*, n. 16.

5. Ibid.

6. John Paul II, address in Korea, May 5, 1984: DC, n. 1876 (1984), p. 612.

7. John Paul II, address in Hiroshima, Feb. 25, 1981: DC, n. 1805 (1981), p. 327.

8. John Paul II, address to UNESCO, n. 10.

9. Ibid., n. 11.

10. John Paul II, address in Hiroshima, n. 4: DC, n. 1805 (1981), pp. 331–32.

11. John Paul II, address to the Pontifical Council for Culture (PCC), Jan. 18, 1983, n. 11: DC, n. 1845 (1983).

12. John Paul II, address to UNESCO, n. 23.

13. Ibid., n. 11.

14. Ibid., n. 12.

15. Ibid., n. 14.

16. Ibid., n. 12.

17. John Paul II, address to PCC, 1984, n. 8: DC, n. 1868 (1984), pp. 189–90.

18. John Paul II, address to UNESCO, n. 9.

19. Paul VI, address to Artists: DC, n. 1425 (1964), cols. 684–90.

20. Paul VI, address of Dec. 7, 1965: DC, n. 1462 (1966), cols. 59–67.

21. Ibid.

22. John Paul II, address in Ravenna: *L'Osservatore Romano*, May 12–13, 1986.

23. Jean Guitton, "Témoignages," in A. Caprioli and L. Vaccaro, eds., *Paolo VI e la Cultura* (Brescia: Morcelliana, 1983), pp. 145–51; see p. 150.

Chapter 4

1. Paul VI, apostolic letter *Octogesima Adveniens*, May 14, 1971, n. 41: DC (*Documentation Catholique*), n. 1587 (1971), pp. 502–13.

2. Letter to Cardinal Casaroli, May 20, 1982: DC, n. 1832 (1982), pp. 604–6.

3. *Octogesima Adveniens*, n. 7.

4. Paul VI, encyclical *Populorum Progressio*, March 26, 1967, n. 1: DC, n. 1492 (1967), cols. 674–704; John Paul II, encyclical *Sollicitudo Rei Socialis*, December 30, 1987.

5. *Populorum Progressio*, nos. 1, 5.

6. Ibid., n. 43.

7. Ibid., n. 80.

8. Ibid., n. 14.

9. Ibid., n. 3.

10. Ibid., n. 42. Here the encyclical cites Father Henri de Lubac.

11. John Paul II, encyclical *Redemptor Hominis*, n. 16: DC, n. 1761 (1979), pp. 304–23.

12. Ibid., n. 15.

13. John Paul II, address to UNESCO, June 2, 1980: DC, n. 1788 (1980), pp. 603–9.

14. John Paul II, opening address at the Puebla Conference, Jan. 28, 1979, n. 14: DC, n. 1758 (1979), pp. 164–72.

15. Ibid., n. 13.

16. Ibid.

17. The relationships between liberation and evangelization will be considered in chapter 7 of this book.

18. *Populorum Progressio*, n. 3.

19. John Paul II, encyclical *Laborem Exercens*, Sept. 14, 1981: DC, n. 1815 (1981), pp. 835–56. The citations that follow in this section come from nn. 2, 3, 10, 27.

20. DC, n. 1805 (1981), pp. 327–30.

21. Vatican II, *Gaudium et Spes*, nn. 64–66.

22. See *Paix et Désarmement, Peace and Disarmament* documents of the World Council of Churches and the Roman Catholic Church. Texts presented by the WCC Commission for International Affairs (Geneva) and the Pontifical Commission "Justice and Peace" (Vatican City). Published in 1982. This citation is on p. 127.

23. Ibid., p. 247.

24. Ibid., p. 249.

25. Ibid., p. 251.

26. Ibid., p. 271.

27. Ibid., p. 273.

28. Ibid., pp. 276–77. The essential connection between peace, ethics, and culture is the continual theme of the annual peace messages issued by the popes since January 1, 1968. The connections between peace and culture are also considered in subsequent chapters of this book. See especially chapter 9 for the responsibilities of those in the arts and sciences.

29. It is very enlightening to reread the section of *Gaudium et Spes* on peace (nn. 77–82) from this standpoint.

30. *L'Osservatore Romano*, Oct. 27–28, 1986.

Chapter 5

1. *Mexico Declaration*, Final Report, World Conference on Cultural Policies (Mexico, July 26–August 6, 1982) (Paris: UNESCO [CLT/MD/1], 1982). See "Mondiacult: Bilan d'une Conférence. Présence catholique" (Paris: Centre Catholique International pour l'UNESCO, 1982). I presented the results of this conference and current trends in cultural policies in my book. *Cultures, notre avenir* (Rome: Gregorian University Press, 1985), chap. 4.

2. John Paul II, encyclical *Laborem Exercens*, Sept. 14, 1981, n. 12: DC (*Documentation Catholique*), n. 1815 (1981), pp. 835–56.

3. Ibid., n. 7.

4. DC, n. 1836 (1982), pp. 804–5.

5. See note 1 in this chapter.

6. John Paul II, address to UNESCO, June 2, 1980, n. 14: DC, n. 1788 (1980), pp. 603–9.

7. *Gaudium et Spes*, n. 73. The question of nonhomogeneous societies will also be treated in chap. 8 when I discuss multicultural societies. John Paul II, *To Build Peace, Respect Minorities*, Message for the World Day of Peace, January 1, 1989; this is the first papal document dedicated to the question of minorities.

8. Paul VI, apostolic exhortation *Evangelii Nuntiandi*, Dec. 8, 1975, n. 30: DC, n. 1689 (1976), pp. 1–22. The relationship between liberation and inculturation is also considered in chap. 7 of this volume. See also H. Carrier, *Cultures, notre avenir*, chap. 6.

9. Paul VI, apostolic letter *Octogesima Adveniens*, May 14, 1971, n. 25: DC, n. 1587 (1971), pp. 502–13.

10. *Gaudium et Spes*, n. 74.

11. Ibid., n. 75.

12. Ibid., n. 74.

13. *Octogesima Adveniens*, n. 25.

14. See the *Charter of the Rights of the Family* published by the Pontifical Council for the Family, Oct. 22, 1983: DC, n. 1864 (1983), pp. 1153–57. Also see *Gaudium et Spes*, n. 52.

15. DC, n. 1878 (1984), pp. 760–62.

16. John Paul II, opening address at the Puebla Conference, Jan. 28, 1979, n. 16: DC, n. 1758 (1979), pp. 164–72.

17. Vatican II, Declaration on Christian Education, *Gravissimum Educationis*, n. 1.

18. DC, n. 1878 (1984), pp. 760–62.

19. Vatican II, Decree on the Media of Social Communication, *Inter Mirifica*, n. 12.

20. DC, n. 1878 (1984), pp. 760–62.

21. *Gaudium et Spes*, n. 59.

22. *Octogesima Adveniens*, n. 25.

23. *Gaudium et Spes*, n. 59.

24. Ibid., n. 75.

25. John Paul II, address to the Pontifical Academy of Sciences: DC, n. 1884 (1984), p. 1052.

26. Ibid. The Council of Europe is seeking a common policy on new problems raised by "Transfontier Television": see the PCC bulletin *Church and Cultures* n. 10 (1988).

27. *Gaudium et Spes*, n. 78. The Church has often upheld defense of the *cultural rights* of individual persons and whole peoples. Those rights would include freedom to create, spread, teach, and undertake research; freedom of information; the free circulation and encounter of persons, and the public expression of their beliefs out of respect for living cultures. For the Church's position see, in particular, the intervention of the Holy See's delegation at the Cultural Forum in Budapest (Oct. 15–Nov. 25, 1985), which brought together the thirty-five countries that had signed the Helsinki Accord: DC, n. 1907 (1985), pp. 1114–17. See my study: DC, n. 1915 (1986), pp. 373–77, and in *Civiltà Cattolica*, Jan. 4, (1986), pp. 82–87.

28. *Mexico Declaration*. See note 1 in this chapter.

29. See H. Carrier, "Comment former les jeunes à l'action culturelle," in *Education, Culture, Evangélisation*, published by the Congregation for Catholic Education and the Pontifical Council for Culture, Rome, 1986, pp. 178–93. There readers will find a brief presentation of pertinent official documents relating to cultural policy: the *Cultural Charter for Africa* (1976), the *European Declaration of Cultural Objectives* (1984), the *Lomé Convention (1975 and 1985), and the Mexico Declaration* (1982).

Chapter 6

1. Paul VI, apostolic exhortation *Evangelii Nuntiandi*, Dec. 8, 1975: DC (*Documentation Catholique*), n. 1689 (1976), pp. 1–22.

2. Ibid., n. 18.

3. John Paul II, to the PCC (Pontifical Council for Culture), Jan. 15, 1985: DC, n. 1890 (1985), pp. 225–26.

4. John Paul II, to the PCC, Jan. 18, 1983, n. 3: DC, n. 1845 (1983), pp. 146–48.

5. Paul VI, *Evangelii Nuntiandi*, n. 20.

6. John Paul II, to the PCC, 1985.

7. John Paul II, to the PCC, 1983, n. 2.

8. John Paul II, encyclical *Dominum et Vivificantem*, May 18, 1986, nn. 56 and 57: DC, n. 1920 (1986), pp. 583–613.

9. Paul VI, *Evangelii Nuntiandi*, n. 26.

10. John Paul II, to UNESCO, June 2, 1980: DC, n. 1788 (1980), pp. 603–9.

11. John Paul II, address to the national congress of the ecclesial movement for cultural involvement, in his letter founding the PCC: DC, n. 1832 (1982), pp. 146–48.

12. Pius XI, to Rev. M.D. Roland-Gosselin, *Semaines sociales de France*, Versailles, 1936, pp. 461–62. Cited in footnote 192 of *Gaudium et Spes*, n. 58.

13. Paul VI, *Evangelii Nuntiandi*, n. 20.

14. Ibid., n. 19.

15. John Paul II, to UNESCO, June 2, 1980, n. 9.

16. See notes 12 and 13 of chap. 2 in this volume. Also see Pius XII, address to Cardinals, Feb. 20, 1946: DC, n. 960 (1945–46), p. 170.

17. Declaration of the Secretariat for Non-Christians, *Attitudes of the Catholic Church toward Believers of Other Religions*, Pentecost 1984: AAS, 76 (1984); see DC, n. 1880 (1984), p. 844.

18. John Paul II, to UNESCO, n. 9.

19. Paul VI, apostolic letter *Octogesima Adveniens*, May 14, 1971, n. 4: DC, n. 1587 (1971), pp. 502–13.

20. Vatican II, *Gaudium et Spes*, n. 43.

21. Ibid., n. 76; see also n. 75.

22. Ibid., n. 92.

23. Paul VI, *Octogesima Adveniens*, n. 50.

24. Vatican II, Decree on the Church's Missionary Activity, *Ad Gentes*, n. 15. See also Vatican II, *Unitatis Redintegratio*, n. 4. and esp. n. 9.

25. Ibid., n. 15.

26. John Paul II, address at Laval University, Quebec, Sept. 9, 1984: DC, n. 1882 (1984), pp. 935–38.

27. John Paul II, to the PCC, 1985.

28. John Paul II, to the PCC, 1984: DC, n. 1868 (1984), pp. 189–90.

29. Ibid.

30. Ibid.

31. John Paul II, letter founding the PCC, May 20, 1982: DC, n. 1832 (1982), pp. 604–6.

32. John Paul II, to the PCC, 1985.

33. John Paul II, Quito address to representatives of the cultural world: DC, n. 1892 (1985), p. 320.

34. P. Vanzan, ed., *Puebla, Comunione e partecipazione* (Rome: AVE, 1979), nn. 2935–36. English-language readers will find the Puebla Final Document, John Paul II's major addresses in Mexico, and useful commentaries in John Eagleson and Philip Scharper, eds., *Puebla and Beyond* (Maryknoll, N.Y.: Orbis Books/USCC, 1979). For a valuable commentary by a Latin American on the importance of cultural considerations and the major contribution of the Puebla Conference, see Marcello de C. Azevedo, *Basic Ecclesial Communities in Brazil: The Challenge of a New Way of Being Church* (Washington, D.C.: Georgetown University Press, 1987), esp. pp. 69–70 and 193–95.

35. P. Vanzan, ed., *Puebla. Comunione e partecipazione*, n. 2999. See also Julio Terán Dutari, "Préambulos para una pastoral de la cultura después de Puebla," *Revista de la Universidad Católica*, Quito, n. 9 (November 1981), pp. 27–39.

36. John Paul II, Quito address to representatives of the cultural world: DC, n. 1892 (1985). To give new impetus to Church activity in the realm of culture, the bishops of Latin America created a "section for culture" within CELAM in 1985. The aims and operational setup of this new organism are presented in the PCC bulletin, *Church and Cultures*, n. 5 (1986). The "evangelization of culture" has been a major theme in the discourses of John Paul II during his visits in Latin American countries: see bulletin *Church and Cultures*, n. 10 (1988).

37. New and greater attention to *cultural conditions* affecting evangelization is clearly evident in recent documents issued by organs of the Holy See. Some of the main ones are listed in the bibliography at the back of this volume, and they are cited at various points in the course of my treatment. Readers might also note the place occupied by the notion of *culture* in the new Code of Canon Law (1983) when it comes to such matters as clerical training, missions, education, and the media of social communication. See canons 248, 787, 793–821, 822–832.

Chapter 7

1. Pedro Arrupe, S.J., Letter of May 14, 1978, in *Ecrits pour Evangéliser*, presented by J.Y. Calvez (Paris: Desclée de Brouwer/Bellarmin, Collection Christus, 1985), pp. 169–75. Other important pronouncements were published by the Orders of the *Carmélites* (1985) and the *Capushins* (1987).

2. *Letter to Diognetus: Patres Apostolici*, Funk ed., 1901, pp. 396–400.

3. *Le Siège apostolique et les Missions* (Paris: Union missionaire du Clergé, 1959).

4. Benedict XV, encyclical *Maximum Illud*, Nov. 30, 1919.

5. Pius XI, encyclical *Rerum Ecclesiae*, Feb. 28, 1926.

6. Robert Redfield, Ralph Linton, and Melville J. Herskovits, "Outline for the Study of Acculturation," *American Anthropologist*, 38 (1936) 149–52. This was a memorandum prepared by the three anthropologists at the request of the Social Research Council, which had asked them to draw a clearer picture of the growing field of studies dealing with "acculturation."

7. There are allusions to it thirty years ago in the writings of Father Pierre Charles, a specialist in missiology, who used the term "acculturation" as a common expression in use. See P. Charles, "Missiologie et acculturation," *Nouvelle Revue Théologique*, 1953, pp. 15–32; idem, *Etudes Missiologiques* (Louvain: Desclée de Brouwer, 1956).

8. See note 14 of this chapter. See also John Paul II, *Catechesi Tradendae*, 1979, n. 53.

9. In 1953 Father Pierre Charles noted that the term "inculturation" had been in use "for about twenty years." See P. Charles, *Etudes Missiologiques*, (1956), p. 137.

10. John Paul II offers a brief *definition* of inculturation that nicely brings out the idea of reciprocity: "Inculturation is the incarnation of the gospel message in autochthonous cultures and, at the same time, the introduction of those cultures into the life of the Church." See his encyclical letter, *Slavorum Apostoli*, for the eleventh centenary of Saints Cyril and Methodius: DC (*Documentation Catholique*), n. 1900 (1985), pp. 717–27; this citation is on p. 724. The document is important for an exploration of the meaning of inculturation and the evangelization of cultures from a historical viewpoint.

11. As I have already indicated, use of the term "inculturation" is quite recent in documents of the Holy See. The first official document to use it was the *Message to the People of God* of the 1977 Synod of Bishops: DC, n. 1731 (1977), p. 1018.

12. 1 Cor 1:22–23.

13. John XXIII, encyclical *Princeps Pastorum*, Nov. 28, 1959, n. 17: DC, n. 1318 (1959), cols. 1537–58.

14. John Paul II, address of April 26, 1979: DC, n. 1764 (1979), p. 455.

15. Paul VI, *Evangelii Nuntiandi*, Dec. 8, 1975, n. 20: DC, n. 1689 (1976), pp. 1–22.

16. Albert Vanhoye, "Nuovo Testamento e inculturazione," in *La Civiltà Cattolica*, n. 3224 (Oct. 20, 1984), pp. 118–36.

17. Vatican II, *Lumen Gentium*, n. 13.

18. John Paul II, address to the Roman Curia, Dec. 22, 1984: DC, n. 1889 (1985), pp. 167–72.

19. *L'Osservatore Romano*, May 1, 1977.

20. Paul VI, address to the symposium of the episcopal conferences of Africa and Madagascar, Sept. 26, 1975: DC, n. 1684 (1975), pp. 853–54.

21. Paul VI, to the Bishops of Asia, Nov. 28, 1970: DC, n. 1576 (1970), pp. 1111–14.

22. John Paul II, address to the Roman Curia: DC, n. 1889 (1985), pp. 167–72. The pope is alluding specifically to n. 13 of *Lumen Gentium*. The extraordinary Synod of 1985 offered this succinct summary of the main aspects of inculturation that we have been examining: "Since the Church is a communion combining unity and diversity through its presence around the world, it assumes whatever it finds

positive in every culture. But inculturation does not mean simply external adaptation; it signifies an inner transformation of authentic cultural values through their integration into Christianity, and the rooting of Christianity in the various human cultures" (Final Report, in DC, n. 1909 [1986], pp. 36–42; this citation is on p. 41).

23. Vatican II, *Ad Gentes*, n. 22.

24. Ibid., n. 11.

25. Vatican II, Constitution on the Sacred Liturgy, *Sacrosanctum Concilium*, n. 37.

26. Quoted by Paul VI, *Evangelii Nuntiandi*, n. 53.

27. *Ad Gentes*, n. 22

28. *Evangelii Nuntiandi*, n. 63.

29. John Paul II, to the PCC (Pontifical Council for Culture), Jan. 18, 1983, n. 4: DC, n. 1845 (1983), pp. 146–48.

30. John Paul II's main addresses on the Christian vocation of Europe would include the following: Gniezno (Poland), June 3, 1979, in DC, n. 1767 (1979); Subiaco (Italy), to the Bishops of Europe, Sept. 28, 1980, in DC, n. 1860 (1980); Santiago de Compostela (Spain), Nov. 9, 1982, in DC, n. 1841 (1982); Vienna (Austria), Sept. 10, 1983, in DC, n. 1860 (1983); Strasbourg (France), to the Council of Europe (Oct. 8, 1988), and the European Parliament (Oct. 11, 1988), in *L'Osservatore Romano*, Oct. 9, 12, 1988. Apostolic Letter, *Egregiae virtutis*, Dec. 31, 1980, designating Saints Cyril and Methodius as co-patrons of Europe, in DC, n. 1801 (1981). The Christian roots of European culture were clearly brought out by the Holy See's delegation to the culture forum in Budapest (Oct. 15–Nov. 25, 1985), which brought together the thirty-five countries that had signed the Helsinki Accord: DC, n. 1911 (1986), pp. 151–52, and *Civiltà Cattolica*, Jan. 4, (1986), pp. 82–87.

31. *Evangelii Nuntiandi*, nn. 27–28.

32. Ibid., n. 27.

33. Ibid., n. 32. These guidelines have often been reiterated by John Paul II, and especially in his opening address at the Puebla Conference. They have also been the subject of two documents issued by the Congregation for the Doctrine of the Faith: *Instruction on a Few Aspects of Liberation Theology*, July 6, 1984, in DC, n. 1881 (1984), pp. 890–900; and *Instruction on Christian Liberty and Liberation*, March 22, 1986, in DC, n. 1916 (1986), pp. 393–412.

34. *Evangelii Nuntiandi*, n. 33. The *Instruction on Christian Liberty and Liberation*, cited in the previous note, clearly stresses the unity and distinction between evangelization and human promotion. On the one hand, "the Church is not departing from its mission" when it speaks out about the promotion of justice in societies. On the other hand, the Church is concerned that "this mission not be absorbed by preoccupations relating to the temporal order or reduced to the latter. That is why the Church takes great care to firmly and clearly maintain both the unity and the distinction between evangelization and human promotion: unity, because it seeks what is good for the whole human being; distinction, because these two tasks enter its mission under different headings" (n. 64). The same instruction deals with "inculturation" from the standpoint of liberation in n. 96.

35. *Evangelii Nuntiandi*, n. 63.

36. International Theological Commission, *Theological Pluralism*, n. 9, 1972; French text in DC, n. 1632 (1973), p. 459. See also its report commemorating the twentieth anniversary of the closing of Vatican II, *Selected Topics of Ecclesiology*; French text in DC, n. 1909 (1986), pp. 57–73. The fourth section of the latter document deals with the theme of "the people of God and inculturation."

37. See *Faith and Inculturation*, document of the International Theological Commission. Vatican, Libreria Editrice Vaticana, 1989.

38. John Paul II, address to the Pontifical Council for Culture, Jan. 13, 1989.

Chapter 8

1. Paul VI, address to the bishops of Africa and Madagascar meeting in Kampala, July 31, 1969: DC (*Documentation Catholique*), n. 1546 (1969), pp. 763–65.

2. Paul VI, message to Africa, *Africae Terrarum*, Oct. 29, 1967: DC, n. 1505 (1967), pp. 1937–56.

3. Declaration of the bishops of Africa and Madagascar present at the fourth Synod of Bishops, Oct. 20, 1974: DC, n. 1664 (1974), pp. 995–96.

4. DC, n. 1435 (1964), pp. 1346–52.

5. Paul VI, *Africae Terrarum*.

6. Paul VI, address of Sept. 26, 1975: DC, n. 1684 (1975), pp. 853–54.

7. Paul VI, address to the bishops of Africa, Oct. 28, 1977: DC, n. 1730 (1977), p. 951.

8. Message of the Church to the Peoples of Africa, Aug. 1, 1969: DC, n. 1546 (1969), pp. 767–70.

9. DC, n. 1787 (1980), pp. 504–5.

10. Ibid.

11. John Paul II, meeting with representatives of the cultural world, Yaoundé, Aug. 13, 1985: DC, n. 1903 (1985).

12. John Paul II, address to priests, religious, and committed persons, Kinshasa, Aug. 15, 1985; *L'Osservatore Romano*, French weekly edition, n. 35.

13. John Paul II, homily in Bangui, Aug. 14, 1985: DC, n. 1903 (1985).

14. John Paul II, homily in Lomé, Aug. 8, 1985: DC, n. 1903 (1985).

15. John Paul II, address to the Cameroon episcopal conference, Aug. 13, 1985: DC, n. 1903 (1985).

16. John Paul II, address to civil authorities and the diplomatic corps, Kinshasa, Aug. 15, 1985; *L'Osservatore Romano*, French weekly edition, n. 35.

17. John Paul II, meeting with representatives of the cultural world, Yaoundé: DC, n. 1903 (1985). The expression recurs frequently during the trip in August 1985.

18. Paul VI, address to Asian bishops in Manila, 1970: DC, n. 1576 (1970), pp. 1111–14.

19. Ibid.

20. Ibid., pp. 1115–19.

21. DC, n. 1526 (1968), p. 1746.

22. DC, n. 1876 (1984), pp. 611–13.

23. Ibid., pp. 615–17.

24. Ibid., pp. 630–32.

25. John Paul II, to the Chinese community in Manila, 1981: DC, n. 1804 (1981), pp. 268–70.

26. Ibid.

27. John Paul II, address at Gregorian University, 1982: DC, n. 1843 (1983), pp. 17–20. This address is the most accurate expression of John Paul II's thinking about the Church's relationship with China.

28. John Paul II, to the bishops of Taiwan, 1984: DC, n. 1871 (1984), pp. 349–50.

29. John Paul II, to the Chinese community in Manila, 1981.

30. John Paul II, address at Gregorian University, 1982: DC, n. 1843 (1983), p. 19.

31. Paul VI's addresses in India were published in the DC, n. 1439 (1965), cols. 1–22.

32. John Paul II's addresses in India were published in the DC, n. 1914 (1986), pp. 283–316.

33. Autograph message of John Paul II to the national conference on culture in India, organized by the All India Association for Christian Higher Education, with the participation of the Pontifical Council for Culture, Bangalore, March 9–16, 1986: DC, n. 1917 (1986), pp. 441–42.

34. DC, n. 1882 (1984), pp. 972–74. John Paul II reiterated these themes in several

of his meetings with native populations during his trip to Canada in September 1984.

35. John Paul II, address to Amerindians of Latin America, Feb. 2, 1985: DC, n. 1892 (1985). See also his talks to Amerindians of Mexico (DC, n. 1758, 1979) and Colombia (DC, n. 1923, 1986).

36. John Paul II, address in Bangkok: DC, n. 1876 (1984), pp. 633–35.

37. Paul VI, address to the diplomatic corps: DC, n. 1735 (1978), p. 103.

38. John Paul II, address to the diplomatic corps in Cameroon, Aug. 12, 1985: DC, n. 1903 (1985).

39. DC, n. 1787 (1980), p. 528.

40. John Paul II, address in Winnipeg (Canada): DC, n. 1882 (1984), pp. 975–76. Here he is citing his encyclical *Redemptor Hominis*, n. 16.

41. John Paul II, address to the bishops of Papua New Guinea and the Solomon Islands: DC, n. 1876 (1984), pp. 624–26.

42. The theme of *inculturation* in the discourses of John Paul II during his visit to the United States (September 10–19, 1987) has been analyzed in the PCC bulletin *Church and Cultures*, n. 9 (1988); see also the pastoral letter of the United States bishops, *The Hispanic Presence: Challenge and Commitment*, A Pastoral Letter on Hispanic Ministry, Dec. 12, 1983, Washington, D.C., National Conference of Catholic Bishops, 1983 (text in English and Spanish). Also see the pastoral letter of the ten black bishops of the United States to the black Catholic community, Sept. 9, 1984: DC, n. 1897 (1985), pp. 583–97.

43. John Paul II, address to the diplomatic corps in Cameroon, Aug. 12, 1985: DC, n. 1903 (1985), p. 908.

44. John Paul II, address to the Indians of Ecuador: DC, n. 1892 (1985).

45. See the periodical *On the Move*, which is published by this pontifical Council, especially n. 46 (1986) devoted to the second world conference on pastoral work relating to emigration (October 1985).

46. These various levels for applying the task of inculturation have often been described by Paul VI and by John Paul II. See, for example: DC. n. 1546 (1969), pp. 763–65; DC, n. 1787 (1980), pp. 504–5; *L'Osservatore Romano*, Nov. 22, 1984. These various areas for inculturation are noted at various points in this volume, especially in the course of this present chapter and the previous one.

Chapter 9

1. *L'Osservatore Romano*, May 9–10, 1983.

2. Vatican II, *Gaudium et Spes*, n. 62.

3. Leo XIII, encyclical *Immortale Dei*, Nov. 1, 1885.

4. Leo XIII, encyclical *Aeterni Patris*, July 4, 1879.

5. Leo XIII, encyclical *Libertas Praestantissimum*, June 20, 1888.

6. See chap. 4.

7. All these citations are from *Gaudium et Spes*, n. 36.

8. Ibid., n. 62.

9. DC (*Documentation Catholique*), n. 1775 (1979), pp. 1009–15. The research and examination proposed by John Paul II have already produced notable results: see Paul Poupard, ed. *Galileo Galilei. Toward a Resolution of 350 Years of Debate—1633–1983*. Pittsburgh, PA, Duquesne University Press, 1983.

10. See note 1 in this chapter.

11. Ibid.

12. DC, n. 1841 (1982), pp. 1098–1101.

13. Ibid.

14. DC, n. 1798 (1980), pp. 1136–40. See Paul Poupard, ed., *Science et foi* (Tournai: Desclée International, 1982).

15. DC, n. 1841 (1982), p. 1100.

16. DC, n. 1798 (1980), p. 1140.

17. John Paul II, address at Santo Tomas University, Manila: DC, n. 1804 (1981), pp. 262–64.

18. DC, n. 1850 (1983), p. 422. John Paul II dealt at length with the responsibility of university personnel in changing cultures when he addressed himself to Jesuit universities. See *L'Osservatore Romano*, Nov. 10, 1985.

19. DC, n. 1805 (1981), p. 327.

20. DC, n. 1864 (1983), pp. 1133–36; see p. 1135. See also his important address to the same academy on the occasion of its fiftieth anniversary: *L'Osservatore Romano*, Oct. 30, 1986.

21. DC, n. 1841 (1982), pp. 1098–1101.

22. John Paul II, address to UNESCO, nn. 20 –22: DC, n. 1788 (1980), pp. 603–9.

23. DC, n. 1864 (1983), p. 1136.

24. Ibid.

25. Ibid.

26. Ibid.

27. Vatican II, *Gaudium et Spes*, n. 62. See Vatican II, Constitution on the Sacred Liturgy, *Sacrosanctum Concilium*, n. 122.

28. DC, n. 1425 (1964), cols. 683–90. The following citations are taken from that same talk.

29. DC, n. 1636 (1973), pp. 660–62.

30. DC, n. 1855 (1983), pp. 655–57.

31. *L'Osservatore Romano*, French weekly edition, July 16, 1985.

32. DC, n. 1859 (1983), pp. 880–81.

33. DC, n. 1767 (1979), p. 613.

34. John Paul II, motu proprio *Quid res Christi geret*, Oct. 3, 1983: DC, n. 1865 (1984), pp. 3–4.

35. John Paul II, address of Feb. 18, 1984: DC, n. 1871 (1984), pp. 351–54.

36. John Paul II, address to artists in Vienna: DC, n. 1860 (1983), pp. 923–25.

37. Vatican II, *Gaudium et Spes*, n. 57.

38. Vatican II, *Inter Mirifica*, n. 7.

39. Vatican II, *Sacrosanctum Concilium*, n. 122.

40. John Paul II, address to Belgian artists: DC, n. 1899 (1985), pp. 689–92.

41. Letter of John Paul II to Msgr. Domenico Bartolucci to mark the celebration of the European Year of Music, on the occasion of the third centenary of Bach, Händel, and Scarlatti, Aug. 6, 1985: DC, n. 1906 (1985), pp. 1060–61.

Main Documents Cited

This bibliography lists the most important documents consulted in the preparation of this book.

Readers should note that the references to Paul VI and John Paul II are simply too numerous to be fully represented in the following list. But they are covered in the notes to the chapters, in accordance with the subject treated.

English-language readers have various sources of translated documents available to them. Besides anthologies of papal, conciliar, and church documents, a valuable ongoing source of current material is *The Pope Speaks* magazine, now published by Our Sunday Visitor Press (200 Noll Plaza, Huntington, Indiana 46750). Its documentation goes back to 1954, when Pius XII was pope.

DOCUMENTS OF VATICAN II

LEO XIII

Encyclicals:
Inscrutabili, April 21, 1878
Aeterni Patris, July 4, 1879
Immortale Dei, Nov. 1, 1885
Libertas Praestantissimum, June 20, 1888
Rerum Novarum, May 15, 1891

BENEDICT XV

Encyclicals:
Ad Beatissimi Apostolorum, Nov. 1, 1914
Maximum Illud, Nov. 20, 1919

PIUS XI

Encyclicals:
Rerum Ecclesiae, Feb. 28, 1926
Divini Illius Magistri, Dec. 31, 1929
Quadragesimo Anno, May 15, 1931
Divini Redemptoris, March 19, 1937
Apostolic Constitution: *Deus Scientiarum Dominus,* May 24, 1931

PIUS XII

Encyclicals:
Summi Pontificatus, Oct. 20, 1939
Evangelii Praecones, June 2, 1951
Radio Messages:
Sept. 1, 1944
Christmas 1944

JOHN XXIII

Encyclicals:
Princeps Pastorum, Nov. 28, 1959
Mater et Magistra, May 15, 1961
Pacem in Terris, April 11, 1963

PAUL VI

Encyclicals:
Ecclesiam Suam, August 6, 1964
Populorum Progressio, March 26, 1967
Message: *Africae Terrarum*, Oct. 29, 1967
Apostolic Letter: *Octogesima Adveniens*, May 14, 1971
Apostolic Exhortation: *Evangelii Nuntiandi*, Dec. 8, 1975

JOHN PAUL II

Encyclicals:
Redemptor Hominis, March 4, 1979
Laborem Exercens, Sept. 14, 1981
Slavorum Apostoli, June 2, 1985
Dominum et Vivificantem, May 18, 1986
Sollicitudo Rei Socialis, Dec. 30, 1987
Apostolic Constitution: *Sapientia Christiana*, April 15, 1979
Apostolic Exhortations:
Catechesi Tradendae, Oct. 16, 1979
Familiaris Consortio,Nov. 22, 1981
Apostolic Letter:
Egregiae Virtutis, Dec. 31, 1980
Mulieris Dignitatem, Aug. 15, 1988
Autograph letter to Cardinal Agostino Casaroli, Secretary of State, on the founding of the Pontifical Council for Culture (PCC): May 20, 1982
Main discourses on Europe: see note 30 of chap. 7
Address to UNESCO: June 2, 1980
Addresses to the Pontifical Council for Culture: Jan. 18, 1983; Jan. 16, 1984; Jan. 15, 1985; Jan. 13, 1986; Jan. 17, 1987; Jan. 15, 1988; Jan. 13, 1989
Main discourses to the Pontifical Academy of Sciences and Scientists: Nov.

10, 1979; Oct. 3, 1981; June 15, 1982; May 9, 1983; Oct. 2, 1984; Oct. 30, 1986; Nov. 7, 1986

Main discourses and texts addressed to university personnel and intellectuals:

1979

Mexico, Jan. 31; I.F.C.U., Rome, Feb. 24; Catholic University of America, Washington, D.C., Oct. 7; Gregorian University, Dec. 15.

1980

Kinshasa, May 4; Catholic Institute of Paris, June 1; Rio de Janeiro, July 1; Urbanian University, Oct. 19; Cologne, Nov. 15.

1981

Salesian University, Jan. 31; University of St. Thomas, Manila, Feb. 18; Hiroshima, Feb. 25; Science and Faith, Rome, April 2.

1982

Ibadan, Nigeria, Feb. 15; Libreville, Feb. 18; Pastoral Ministry in Universities, Rome, March 8; Bologna, April 18; Augustinianum, May 8; Coimbra, May 15; Padua, Sept. 12; Salamanca, Nov. 1; Madrid, Nov. 3; Palermo, Nov. 20.

1983

Guatemala, March 7; Milan, May 22; Cracow, June 22; Vienna, Sept. 12; FUCI-MEIC, Rome, Dec. 3.

1984

Bari, Feb. 26; Seoul, May 5; Fribourg, June 13; Sacred Heart University, Milan, Sept. 6; Laval University, Quebec, Canada, Sept. 9; Pavia, Nov. 3.

1985

MEIC, Rome, Feb. 9; Leuven, May 20; Louvain-la-Neuve, May 21; Yaoundé, Aug. 13; Nairobi, Aug. 18; Jesuit Universities, Nov. 9.

1986

New Delhi, Feb. 2; Poona, Feb. 10; Bangalore, March 9; Lyons, Oct. 7; Florence, Oct. 18.

SYNODS OF BISHOPS

Messages and reports of the synods of 1971, 1977, and 1985

CONGREGATION FOR THE DOCTRINE OF THE FAITH

Instruction on a Few Aspects of Liberation Theology: July 6, 1984
Instruction on Christian Liberty and Liberation: March 22, 1986

SECRETARIAT FOR NON-CHRISTIANS

Attitudes of the Catholic Church toward Believers of Other Religions: June 10, 1984
Pastoral Attention to African Traditional Religion, March 25, 1988

PONTIFICAL COUNCIL FOR THE FAMILY

Charter of the Rights of the Family: Oct. 22, 1983

INTERNATIONAL THEOLOGICAL COMMISSION
Theological Pluralism: 1972
Selected Topics of Ecclesiology: 1985
Faith and Inculturation: 1989

Index